The Only Sales Guide You'll Ever Need

The Lost Art of Closing:
Winning the Ten Commitments That Drive Sales

EAT THEIR LUNCH

EAT
THEIR
LUNCH

Winning Customers Away from Your Competition

ANTHONY IANNARINO

PORTFOLIO/PENGUIN

Portfolio/Penguin
An imprint of Penguin Random House LLC
375 Hudson Street
New York, New York 10014

Most Portfolio books are available at a discount when purchased in quantity for sales promotions or corporate use. Special editions, which include personalized covers, excerpts, and corporate imprints, can be created when purchased in large quantities. For more information, please call (212) 572-2232 or e-mail specialmarkets@penguinrandomhouse.com. Your local bookstore can also assist with discounted bulk purchases using the Penguin Random House corporate Business-to-Business program. For assistance in locating a participating retailer, e-mail B2B@penguinrandomhouse.com.

LIBRARY OF CONGRESS CATALOGING-IN-PUBLICATION DATA

Names: Iannarino, Anthony, author.
Title: Eat their lunch : winning customers away from your competition / Anthony Iannarino.
Description: New York City : Portfolio, 2018.
Identifiers: LCCN 2018029804 (print) | LCCN 2018033958 (ebook) | ISBN 9780525537632 (ebook) | ISBN 9780525537625 (hardback)
Subjects: LCSH: Selling. | Competition. | BISAC: BUSINESS & ECONOMICS / Sales & Selling. | BUSINESS & ECONOMICS / Development / Business Development.
Classification: LCC HF5438.25 (ebook) | LCC HF5438.25 .I2496 2018 (print) | DDC 658.8/04—dc23
LC record available at https://lccn.loc.gov/2018029804

Printed in the United States of America
10 9 8 7 6 5 4 3 2 1

Book design by Daniel Lagin

This book is dedicated to the women and men who compete to help their clients produce better results, working to win new business from their competitors while also doing what is necessary to protect their clients from competitive threats.

This book is dedicated to those who compete with a set of nonnegotiable values built on character, honesty, and integrity, those who will not do "whatever it takes" because their desire to win includes an unwillingness to compromise these values. It's dedicated to those who are brave enough to lose with honor and who have the persistence to try again.

This book is dedicated to the people who sell in competitive industries where things are mostly equal, and where the value they create is the primary differentiator; those who don't have the advantage of having a solution that is so much in demand that they can simply take orders.

Contents

PART 2
BUILDING CONSENSUS: WIRE THE BUILDING

PART 3
WINNING WITH THE INTANGIBLES

Foreword

I GREW UP IN AN INSANELY COMPETITIVE INDUSTRY. THE SER-
vice I sold was highly profitable, but it wasn't sexy. It was perceived and
treated as a commodity by most buyers. And since virtually all of those
buyers were already using the service sold, the only way to win was by
taking those accounts from entrenched, incumbent vendors who were in-
tent on holding onto their lucrative business.

"You guys are all the same" was the regular refrain from buyers who
perceived no difference between the various vendors in my niche. Most
preferred to avoid meeting altogether and brushed off appointment requests with "Just give me your best price; if you're in the ballpark, we'll talk."

The race to the bottom on a pure price play in this hypercompetitive
environment was short, fast, and usually ended abruptly—incumbents did
not lose accounts on price.

To call it a grind is an understatement. Every opportunity was a chess
match. Outhustle was the name of the game. There was no easy button.
Each deal had to be EARNED. In this grueling, cutthroat, winner-takes-
all world, salespeople who found it difficult to differentiate beyond price
burned out quickly.

It was inside this crucible that I learned how to master the board and eat their lunch. If you could flip the commodity script on its ear. If you could deftly expose competitor weaknesses. If you could connect emotionally with buyers and influence their behaviors. If you were adept at displacing competitors. You could make a ton of money.

I loved this world and thrived in it. Displacing fat and happy and often lazy competitors who were taking advantage of my prospects was a game I lived for. Shifting a perceived commodity to a differentiated value-added service was like creating fine art.

What made me successful, along with many other professionals who work in similar competitive situations, was not manipulation, tricks, or technology. It wasn't an overwhelming competitive advantage. It certainly wasn't marketing, branding, or advertising.

Instead, it was making the process of buying personal. It was professionalism, integrity, and an intense focus on human relationships. When I mastered human-influence frameworks, deal strategy, and my own emotions, I rose above the pack. When I became a problem solver who focused on delivering measurable business outcomes, I won the day—again and again and again.

In this masterpiece book, for the first time, Anthony Iannarino teaches you the art and science of competitive displacement. He shows you step by step how the very best salespeople in the world obliterate their fiercest competitors. You'll learn winning strategies and frameworks that will instantly allow you to differentiate yourself in the crowded global marketplace.

Anthony and I are like brothers from another mother. He's one of my very best friends. We talk about sales and selling constantly. Obsessively. Sometimes several times in a day. At times we debate, argue, and disagree on an approach or an idea, but we are both driven in our collective mission to advance sales as a profession.

We are also in violent agreement that the sales profession has gotten soft and that salespeople have lost their competitiveness. Far too many salespeople want the deal handed to them on a silver platter. As Anthony says, we have moved from a generation of rainmakers to a new era of rain barrels who stare at the sky hoping that something might fall in.

I've got news for you, hope is not a strategy, and it's time for an awakening from this sad malaise that has descended on the sales profession. It begins with this book.

Why should you pay attention to Anthony? He has lived in and continues to live in the trenches just like you. He grinds it out with his own sales team—skipping meals and doing deals. Like so many great sales professionals who do hand-to-hand combat and consistently come out winners, he's clear, to the point, and filters out all of the fluffy BS so that you can get to the truth.

In *Eat Their Lunch*, Anthony holds nothing back. You are going to get the unadulterated truth about why you are failing and not reaching your income goals. It will become crystal-clear why your competitors always seem to be getting the best of you.

With the turn of each page, though, you'll gain more confidence in competitive situations. You'll employ new strategies that give you a decisive edge. You'll learn how to interact with buyers who think you are a commodity and will flip the script. When you put Anthony's techniques to work in your sales day, you will win big, your prospects will win big, and you will eat your competitors' lunch.

So now you have a decision to make. You can send this book back for a refund, open your mouth, tilt your head to the sky, and hope for the best. Or you can take action and learn from one of the great masters of the sales profession and become the rainmaker you were destined to be.

Jeb Blount, author of *Fanatical Prospecting,*
People Buy You, Sales EQ, and *Objections*

A Word to the Reader

THIS IS MY THIRD BOOK IN AS MANY YEARS. LIKE THE FIRST two, *The Only Sales Guide You'll Ever Need* and *The Lost Art of Closing: Winning the Ten Commitments That Drive Sales*, this book is a field manual of sorts. You can think of it as an operating manual or a playbook. It isn't a book of theories that gives you only a conceptual framework. It is written so that you can take action on what you read and displace your competitors inside your dream client accounts.

Much of what is contained in this book is easy to understand and difficult to execute. That said, only charlatans sell the idea that you should be able to have what you want without real effort on your part. What lies between the covers of this book is the real work you have to do to create and win opportunities in clients that are presently held by your competitors. I offer no shortcuts, no tricks, and no easy answers. Instead, I offer you a strategy for increased effectiveness and results in trade for your effort.

Some of what is included here are difficult concepts that I have worked to make simple, so they can be used in a way that gives you choices. Good salesmanship is made up of good choices. You will read everything in this book through your own experience, meaning you are seeing what is written here through a certain lens. This book will provide you with a new set of lenses through which to see the problem of displacing your competitor, your role as a salesperson, sales manager, or sales leader, and your view of your dream clients.

This book will also leave you with questions. You'll ask yourself, "What is the right idea to share to get my client's attention?," "How can I create more value in this relationship?," and "How do I change the impression of my company with someone who might have had a bad experience with us in the past?" These are situational questions that you will need to answer, and the answers will vary from person to person and company to company. But these are the questions that produce better results.

Finally, I want to say a word about the order in which I produced these books. I wrote *The Only Sales Guide You'll Ever Need* to provide salespeople with a competency model, a set of mind-sets (character traits) and skill sets necessary to succeed in sales now. That book is about how you become a person worth buying from. The second book, *The Lost Art of Closing*, is about the commitments we need to help clients make in order to produce new and better results. This book is a methodology for creating and winning new business by displacing your competitors, something necessary for most of us in sales, and something rarely spoken about. This book completes the trilogy, building on the prior two books and providing a framework for winning new business in a competitive marketplace.

EAT THEIR LUNCH

Introduction

DO YOU KNOW THE FEELING, AS A SALESPERSON, OF HAVING A completely new and groundbreaking product to sell, having a list of prospective client companies that desperately need what you're selling because no one else sells it, and closing a series of large, lucrative deals in quick succession with no real effort on your part? Neither do I.

Most of us work in mature industries that are overcrowded, where we are perceived as commodities (even when we are not), and where competition is ferocious. We work in industries where growth requires capturing market share from our competitors, and in many cases requires that we take their clients from them while they attempt to take our clients from us. How else do you grow by 12 percent in an industry that is growing by 2.7 percent annually?

A Blue Ocean Strategy* is a framework for creating new markets where there is no competition. It moves a company from being forced to compete against aggressive rivals, and it improves growth opportunities and profitability. Companies like Netflix, Uber, and Airbnb, among others,

---

* *Blue Ocean Strategy: How to Create Uncontested Market Space and Make the Competition Irrelevant* is a popular book by W. Chan Kim and Renée Mauborgne.

all created blue oceans. They disrupted their industry with an offering that—for a time—made them a category of one, eliminating the necessity of having to compete against other companies and avoiding commoditization. As much as you would love to work in a blue ocean and create new markets where there is little competition, high profit margins, and easy growth, the world you live in is quite the opposite. If you picked up this book, you work and sell in that part of the ocean where the water is deeply and abundantly red. This is a book about how to live, thrive, and survive in a red ocean. It's a framework for competing against tough and worthy rivals. It's about competing for their existing clients by creating greater value. If the ocean is red, it doesn't have to be your blood that stains the water.

Over the past decade or so, ideas about what selling is and how it should be done have been changed by the advent of technology. The rise of inbound marketing, the strategy of creating content that generates warm, ready-to-buy leads (something with much in common with a unicorn) has led salespeople to believe that they are not responsible for prospecting and creating new opportunities and that they can simply be a "social seller," connecting with contacts in hope of creating an opportunity without having to interrupt them. This means many salespeople have also abandoned the responsibility of being trusted advisers in their own right. Many sales leaders are determined to automate opportunity creation through email, sending contacts emails that appear to be from a salesperson, ruining the medium by making all email from salespeople suspect— and preventing the salespeople from developing relationships through real communication.

The sales organizations that have followed this advice have lost their way. They are confused, frustrated, and experiencing a lack of new opportunities and the growth that accompanies them. In addition, I've noticed that under this approach, salespeople lose motivation and go through the motions without working to create opportunities, win those opportunities, and help their dream clients produce better results through their effort.

What is needed now is a playbook for displacing your competitors and growing market share in a red ocean. To create and win new opportunities, you must be able to make a difference in a crowded, "me-too" market. That difference has to be the greater value you can create for dream clients, and that requires a more substantial, more compelling, and more strategic level of value.

This book is a clarion call to push things back toward the fundamentals that sales and selling are built on. Those fundamentals include creating value, capturing mindshare, proactively prospecting, and working to displace your competitors from your dream client companies. It's also a reminder that sales is a competition and you are a competitor. It's often a zero-sum game where your win is someone else's loss. You have to pour your heart and soul into the game, and bring your best self to the endeavor of winning new business. This book is the strongest of nudges to act with urgency. Or, as one early reader framed it, "I am going to make sure that this book is not available on the bookshelves in my city, so my competitors never get to read it." In the same spirit, this book will show you how to seek and maintain a competitive advantage.

ON COMPETITION

Before we can talk about displacing your competitors and eating their lunch, we have to discuss how you should be thinking about your competition. Lest you think effective competitive displacement is about taking a bloodthirsty, "whatever it takes," "win at all costs" approach to sales, allow me to dispel any such notions.

Your company goes out into the market to win new clients. You believe that what you sell—and how you sell it—is better than what your competitors sell. Your intention is to better serve those companies and customers that are not getting what they really want or need. When this is true, you win clients from your competitors and you capture market share. Your competitors, meanwhile, aren't sitting passively, losing market share without so much as a response. Instead, they are paying attention to what you are doing to create more value and developing ways to create even greater value. They take their new offering to the market and target your clients with the offer of greater value, in turn competitively displacing you (or trying to).

The beneficiaries of such competition are the consumers. We produce better offerings, and the customers we serve get better results because of our competition to create greater value and win their business. This is how business evolves and things get better. It's why you don't have a Nokia phone or a BlackBerry sitting next to you as you read this book.

Your integrity is a critical factor in competing successfully over the long term. Nothing in this book will teach you that you need to win at all costs. You should never compete by doing anything that is illegal or immoral, and you should never put your name or character at risk. There is also nothing between the front and back covers of this book that suggests that you "crush the competition" or perceive your competitor as "your enemy." You are not a Mafia don or a warlord out to destroy your rivals. Behaving that way ultimately makes you someone who is difficult to trust and impossible to see as a long-term partner. Very little of what leads to successfully taking your competitors' clients has anything to do with your competitors themselves. Instead, you will win those clients by creating greater value than they do, which is the only sustainable strategy for winning clients.

Dealing with Dirty Tricks

Even today, some salespeople rely on old-school, tactical approaches and high-pressure techniques to win sales. Some are still being taught that success requires a "whatever it takes" attitude, approaching sales as something they are doing to someone. This approach and the tactics it requires are outmoded and ineffective, and so are the strategies these salespeople use to compete and win.

You don't win by focusing on your competition. What makes you a dangerous competitor is how *you* play the game. Let's start by eliminating the things that your competitors routinely do in an attempt to cause you problems and take your business, the things that make them weak competitors.

Some of your competitors compete on price alone, offering a poorer service than you do at a lower price point, while falsely promising the same results you can offer. They will win the most price-sensitive customers in the market, many of whom will live with their shortcomings for much longer than you might imagine. While these competitors usually win clients who perceive only the lowest price as value, they will occasionally win good clients, clients who will stick with them until you find a way to displace them. Know that you cannot do anything about a competitor with an irrational pricing structure. It doesn't change your pricing model or strategy, so your only response should be to compete in a way that allows you to win with a higher price. That means creating greater value (something you will learn to do in the following chapters).

One extremely aggressive competitor made the price play by sending an unsolicited quote to my client, providing them with a savings analysis based on what they believed to be my company's pricing. They sent a letter to every executive in the company, and the savings they proposed were significant. There was nothing I could do to stop them from sending the unsolicited price proposal. Fortunately, the value we created was worth more than what my client could save by switching to my competitor.

You have competitors who will make negative statements about you and your company that are completely untrue in an attempt to win business. This has happened to me many times, including one competitor who called a client of twenty years to suggest that my company was going bankrupt when in fact we were having a record year on both top- and bottom-line growth. My client called to tell me what the competitor said, but because of our honest and transparent relationship, the call was to make us aware, not because they believed our sketchy competitor.

The only thing you can do about competitors who go negative to sell against you is to ensure that when they say something negative it is so different from who you are known to be that the incongruity causes your competitor to immediately lose credibility. If your prospective client questions you about anything they may have said, you say, "I have no idea why they would say something like that. I am sure they are confused. If you have any concern here, I will address it for you completely."

I've also had competitors who provided kickbacks to contacts within the companies whose business we were competing for. They were willing to win at any cost, even violating their company's code of ethics and allowing the contacts to put themselves in a precarious position within their own company by taking money in exchange for their business. In one instance, I found out about a competitor's kickbacks when the client contacts receiving them asked me during a negotiation what my company could do for them personally. We walked away.

When confronted with the choice of doing something illegal or immoral to win business or walking away, walk away. There is no deal that is worth your integrity or your character. Those who do something illegal or immoral to win business are not competing—they are acting outside of competition, avoiding competition. They might have some short-term wins, but over the longer term you will see them fade away. More important, you don't want anyone who is dishonest enough to steal from their own company as your client.

In a less nefarious approach, I once had a competitor who delivered coffee and doughnuts to my client every Friday morning. Fortunately, doughnuts are no longer the kind of value that compels change.

How You Speak About Your Competitors

While your competitors may use every opportunity to say negative things about you, how should you talk about them, those you are going to displace? No matter who the competitor, how bad they are, whether they do things that are illegal or immoral, and no matter if you find their business practices to be irrational, you cannot speak negatively about them directly. In fact, you should do the opposite.

Let me explain: When salespeople attempt to displace competitors who are undercutting them on price, I've noticed that they often say, "Their pricing is irrational. There is no way they are making a profit. They can't run a business with that model." There is a lot to unpack here. First, the salesperson may be correct in their assessment that their competitor's lower price indicates that they are allowing their client to underinvest in the results they need, or that their competitor's pricing isn't profitable or sustainable. However, the fact remains that they have clients, meaning they are producing some results. Second, it's hard for you as an external observer to say anything definitive about your competitor's profitability, especially when they may have been in business for longer than your own business. The idea that they are not a safe choice is difficult to sell when there is no real evidence of their impending demise.

Finally, and perhaps most important, trying to create doubt about your competitor doesn't do much to create a preference for your solution.

In fact, if you have to point the bony finger of indignation at your competitor, it looks like you have little to offer in terms of differentiation or greater value.

There aren't a lot of good reasons to bring up your competitors in a sales conversation, even when you are speaking with their existing client, your dream client. Even though the conversations we have are about a current state that is insufficient and the better future state they desire, it doesn't matter which of your many competitors is failing to deliver that future state. The fact of the matter is that they aren't producing a result the client needs now—or one that the client doesn't even know is available to them. You don't need to speak poorly about your competitor to create a compelling case for change. Instead, these conversations are fueled by your knowledge of where you create greater value than your competitors and the common challenges your value proposition is designed to solve. You also have ideas about what their future challenges will be, something we'll cover in great detail in chapter 2.

If and when you have to speak about your competitor, there is a better way to do so, and one that does more to position you as a professional, a trusted adviser, and someone who has a better offering. Instead of trying to tear your competitor down, if you are asked about them, you say something positive. You say, "We have friends there. They're good people, and they do some really good work in some scenarios. That said, we have wildly different ideas about how to serve our clients and the results that we produce. Can I share with you what we do differently and why?" Because you are continually meeting with prospects, and through your ongoing work with existing clients, you should always be gaining new knowledge about what you do differently. This approach is professional, as it doesn't require you to say anything negative about the competitor at all. It's professional to know people in the industry without suggesting that they are your sworn enemy or incompetent or evil. By saying something nice about your competitor, you establish yourself as a professional. When you say,

"We have wildly different ideas . . . ," you open up a conversation about what makes you different, why you do certain things differently from your competitors, and how it produces better results. This is one of the outcomes you need to sell effectively, namely differentiation that creates greater value and a preference to work with you. You say, "The industry tends to believe that this is the right way to do this one thing. We have found that there is a better way to do it." You never even have to mention the competitor by name.

You will have clients who speak ill of your competitor when they are dissatisfied with their work. Their complaints sound like music to your ears because you know that the unhappier the client, the more compelled they are to change. I want to caution you against taking the bait and piling on when your prospective client invites you to confirm their negative opinion of your competitor. A prospect who shares a long list of your competitor's high crimes and misdemeanors may not be sharing a truthful and accurate view of your competitor's role in their unhappiness. In fact, their complaints may mask the fact that their dissatisfaction is not because of your competitor's failings, but because of the client's own stubbornness, refusing to take your competitor's advice to make necessary changes. If you are being honest with yourself, you know you have clients like this, too.

Finally, you need to let go of beliefs about your competitors that get in your way when it comes to selling effectively. Believing that your competitors lie and that their approach or pricing model is responsible for your losses is unhealthy. It is disempowering because it absolves you of the responsibility of knowing how to position yourself, your company, and your solution as creating the kind of differentiated, compelling value that would have beaten them. It's your job to get the client to perceive the value you create, and it is that perception that allows you to win. If you hold yourself responsible for a loss, you can change your approach and improve. If you blame your competitors, you absolve yourself of responsibility—and you continue to lose.

You cannot do anything about your competitor. Nothing you say or do will make them change their behavior, their approach, or their pricing. Even when you start to win their clients by creating greater value, your competitors are likely to respond by doubling down on their existing practices, so your focus has to shift to improving how you sell. That doesn't mean believing the platitude that goes, "I don't want to be better than anyone else. I just want to be better than I was yesterday." While that sounds nice, your goal should be to be better than you were yesterday *and* better than your best competitor today.

With all that said, what I'll show you in this book is how to play fair while making your competitors feel like you have an unfair advantage. You'll create such a strong preference for your solution that they feel like it's an unfair fight.

How to Have an Unfair Advantage

When it comes to watching sports or any other competitive endeavor, we like the idea of a fair fight between evenly matched opponents. When you compete in sales, however, you want things to be unequal and tilted deeply in your direction. Your character and integrity are integral components of your competitive advantage, so you are not going to sacrifice them in order to seek some other advantage. As you'll discover in this book, when it comes to selling effectively over the long term, who you are matters more than what you sell. You will create an unfair advantage by being better at creating a compelling case for change and by selling better than your competitors.

In Part One of this book, **Developing Relationships and Gaining Access,** you will discover how to develop the new relationships you need to begin the process of creating an opportunity for displacement—in other words, eat their lunch.

In **Chapter 1: You Are the Value Proposition,** you'll learn that your product, your service, and your solution are likely not enough to create a case for change or a preference to work with you. Instead, your ability to step into the role of trusted adviser will allow you to create compelling, differentiated value and begin the process of displacing your competitors. To do this, you are going to begin the relationship from the highest level of value, something we call Level 4, where change begins, instead of the lower levels that identify you as a commodity.

In **Chapter 2: Capturing Mindshare**, you will create competitive advantage by developing your business acumen and situational knowledge and putting it to work helping your dream clients understand why they need to do something different and shaping how they decide to take action. The person who controls the lens through which the client views their business and their challenges is the person who creates and wins opportunities.

Chapter 3: Creating an Opening Through Nurture Campaigns and Pursuit Plans provides a blueprint for putting your insights to work developing the case for change and becoming known for your ability to create a better future state. It takes time to create opportunities, and this plan will guide you.

All of these insights are for naught if you don't put them to work by prospecting. In **Chapter 4: Prospecting with the Intention of Displacement**, you will build a prospecting plan that allows you to create an opportunity inside your competitor's account.

In **Part Two: Building Consensus: Wire the Building**, you'll learn a new framework for creating opportunities and building the support necessary to win a takeaway.

Chapter 5: Helping Your Dream Clients Discover Something About Themselves will provide you with a new, different way to think about discovery, one that allows you to understand how to create real change. You will learn a lot about your clients, and quite a bit about yourself here as well.

Chapter 6: Creating Opportunities is a deeper dive into the creation of real opportunities as proven by the client's commitment to move forward with the process. This chapter will remind you that sales is one part opportunity creation and one part opportunity capture. Displacements begin with the creation of an opportunity.

Chapter 7: Building Consensus Horizontally and Vertically and the chapter that follows, **Chapter 8: Finding a Path to a Deal**, are designed to help you understand the map that is your dream client stakeholders and their relationships to find a path forward.

This brings us to **Part Three: Winning with the Intangibles,** with four chapters that help you position yourself as the right person to buy from. Forever.

Chapter 9: Creating a Preference is a list of strategies that tip the balance in your favor in a contest between you and your competitor. If you are going to steal business, your dream client will have to prefer to have you on their team, instead of their existing partner.

Chapter 10: Becoming a Trusted Adviser and Consultative Salesperson provides a recipe you can follow to be both. Everyone aspires to be their client's trusted adviser; here you will learn how to achieve that goal.

In **Chapter 11: Developing an Executive Presence,** you are now the value proposition, and that means you need to look and act like a peer. If you are going to lead change, you have to look like a leader.

Chapter 12: How to Build a Wall of Fire Around Your Clients tells you how to prevent what is in this book from happening to you! (And it will keep you from having to steal all the copies of this book from your local bookstore.)

The **Conclusion: Parting Thoughts** is just that, a few ideas about the great game of sales and what it means to those of us who play it every day.

PART 1

DEVELOPING RELATIONSHIPS AND GAINING ACCESS

Chapter 1

YOU ARE THE VALUE PROPOSITION

IF YOU ARE GOING TO DISPLACE YOUR COMPETITOR (I.E., EAT their lunch), you'll have to make it worth your dream client's time, energy, and money to change. You'll also have to compel them to change.

Right now you may be infected with the belief that you simply need to wait for some negative event to cause your dream client to change. You may believe that your competitor must fail and fail badly, disrupting your prospective client's business before they will seriously consider changing partners. You may hope that some event occurs that causes them to search their email to find your contact information or sift through the stack of business cards in their junk drawer.

But waiting isn't a strategy. Waiting is much too passive, much too reactive. A strategy to win new clients requires that you are more proactive and disciplined in your approach. It also means you understand that right now, while you are reading this very page, some of your dream clients are unhappy with their current provider. Maybe not so unhappy that they are going to fire their current provider today or tomorrow, but they are struggling to produce the results they need and they want things to be better. Let's look at why your dream client may be susceptible to change now.

SOME SIGNS THAT A DISPLACEMENT IS LIKELY

Before we get into the overall strategy for a competitive displacement, let's explore some of the signs that a displacement is possible—or even likely. If you have ever had the experience of being displaced, some of these will ring a rather unpleasant bell.

Complacency

If there is a root cause of all displacements, it's complacency. Having won the client's business and served them for years, your competitor falls into a routine with your dream client. The problem that allowed your competitor to win their dream client was long ago solved, and for years your competitor has simply continued to execute the solution that solved that problem.

But over time, the outside world has continued to change. Your competitor's client (the one you are going to steal away from them) has started to experience new challenges, challenges that their current partner has left unaddressed. The client now has increased competition, some of which is coming from lower-priced competitors. They have increased customer demands they have been unable to fulfill. They have systemic challenges that have gone unresolved long enough that they have accepted that their current workarounds are all that can be done, even if they are increasingly ineffectual.

When your competitor gives up working to create new value because they've grown complacent, they are exposed to a competitive displacement (and the same applies to you and your clients).

A Sense of Entitlement

When your competitor has served their client for years—maybe even decades—they believe that their relationship creates an impenetrable boundary that repels all potential rivals, like a force field. They believe their history of working together entitles them to their client's business in perpetuity. This is a sort of soft arrogance that leads to complacency.

In another form of entitlement that gives rise to a displacement, your competitor believes that their contractual relationship is enough to protect the business, that their client won't change before the contract expires. To believe that a contract will prevent you from losing your client's business is to be woefully unaware of how little protection a contract offers or just how little you are entitled to their business. In fact, comfort with the status quo and the cost of changing partners are often stronger barriers to change than contractual commitments. The client's patience often expires before their contract does.

When your competitor feels a sense of entitlement, their overconfidence can create an opportunity for displacement.

Apathy and Lack of Communication

Complacency and a sense of entitlement can also manifest as apathy, resulting in a failure to communicate frequently and meaningfully with the client. After years working with a company, your competitor can fall into a comfortable routine, where their client doesn't ask any more of them and they don't bring new ideas. What little communication there is turns into a "check-in" call where no real value is created for the client.

Over time, the relationship between your competitor and your dream client grows stale and becomes vulnerable to internal and external threats. Your competitor's apathy gets reflected in their client's apathy toward them and their relationship. Meanwhile you, the salesperson who has been consistently and persistently asking for a meeting while showing a serious interest in the business, become a lot more interesting to the client, opening up the possibility of a displacement.

Resentment

After serving them for a long time, some salespeople start to resent their clients. You may or may not have witnessed this in yourself or in your organization. The client starts to become sort of an annoyance, taking more time than is necessary and becoming needier. I have seen companies that claim to be client-focused do nothing but complain about their clients. While that resentment may only be expressed internally, it is a mistake to think your client doesn't feel the change in your relationship. When your competitor no longer treats your dream client as the most important and interesting thing in the world, they've created an opportunity for displacement.

New Stakeholders

When a new stakeholder holding a position of power enters the scene, things can get interesting. Why? What's the first thing a new leader or manager wants to do upon starting their new role? They want to change something. They want to start making a name for themselves, establish their authority, and get an easy win on the scoreboard.

One of the easiest ways they can make an impact is by removing a partner who is complacent, who feels entitled to the business because they have a contract, who has not made the changes they've been asked to make, who no longer communicates, and who is doing nothing about the systemic challenges to the business. There might be a few people who are upset when their current provider gets a pink slip and is replaced, but even those with deep relationships tend to get over it pretty quickly.

I've personally lost a client because a new stakeholder didn't like our model and believed the best thing she could do would be to replace my company with the lowest-price competitor in that particular market. The quality declined and the challenges we had successfully addressed all resurfaced. Within a year she was gone, and we were back. But it wasn't just the poor results that caused the company to bring us back in; it was a new stakeholder taking the role when the person who removed us was herself removed.

Long-Unaddressed Needs and Changes

When your dream client has asked their partner to make changes to address their needs and is ignored for months and years, they are ripe for a displacement. There are two factors at work here. First, no one likes to be ignored. The more time passes and the more requests they need to make for some necessary change, the closer they are to switching to a partner who can address their needs in a timely manner. Second, not making the changes is an indication that one does not care. If your competitor cared, they'd be trying to do something different and having conversations about what things they are changing and how they are doing it to meet their client's need.

You know this idea as "dissatisfaction" or "pain," the common vernacular in sales that suggests the client has a compelling need to change. It's what you have been taught to explore in a discovery meeting so that you can come up with a solution that addresses the areas in which your dream client is unhappy and needs things to be different. This used to be the gold standard in competitive displacement strategy, but at the time this book is being published, this is no longer true. Instead, your dream clients in many cases have learned to live with the status quo, lowered their standards, and find it difficult to consider changing when doing so brings only marginal improvement. They may want to avoid the risk of changing only to end up with a different or unknown set of challenges.

Unaddressed Systemic Challenges

All the factors listed above weaken your competitor's hold on their client and can improve your chances of motivating your dream client to change their provider. But if you think about these factors you will quickly realize that you yourself are guilty of many of these crimes against your clients, and yet you still have their business (not to worry, we'll do something about all of these risk factors in chapter 12). The truth is that many of these factors aren't always enough to compel change, which is why companies don't make these changes even when they should.

The first third of this book is about developing and gaining relationships that allow you to capture mindshare and create a compelling case for change by leveraging the threats to the business that come from huge, tectonic shifts that, left unaddressed, will eventually cause the business harm. If the needs left unaddressed by your competitor answer the "What keeps you up at night" question that you would ask the client, then the systemic threats provide you with a case for "This is what *should* be keeping you up at night."

The factors discussed above begin a displacement based on identified client wants and needs and put you in a position where you are reacting to the causes of change that already exist. The approach we are taking here, one of addressing the strategic or systemic threats that are largely being ignored, creates a compelling case for change that is proactive. The approach in this book is not one where you wait for a client to decide they need to change; instead, you are going to compel that change. This is a good place to introduce what your dream client needs from you, something we'll explain by contrasting it with what they are getting now. To do this work, we'll have to look at how most sales organizations and salespeople operate now to discover the difference in approach that compels change and creates the opportunity to displace your competitors.

ENTERING FROM THE RIGHT: THE FOUR LEVELS OF VALUE CREATION

There are four levels of value you can create for your clients. While most salespeople create lower levels of value, you will create a higher, more strate-

L4VC OVERVIEW

 **PRODUCT**

⊕ GOOD PRODUCT OR SERVICE

⊖ UNDIFFERENTIATED
DOES NOT GENERATE LOYALTY
COMMODITIZED

L-2 SERVICE

⊕ OUTSTANDING SERVICE
OUTSTANDING SUPPORT
GOOD PRODUCT OR SERVICE

⊖ NOT ENOUGH FOR B2B
NOT PROACTIVE

L-3 BUSINESS RESULTS

⊕ SOLVES TANGIBLE BUSINESS PROBLEMS
OUTSTANDING SERVICE & SUPPORT
GOOD PRODUCT OR SERVICE

⊖ PRONE TO LOSS THROUGH DISSATISFACTION
COMMODITIZED

 **STRATEGIC PARTNER**

⊕ STRATEGIC OUTCOMES
ENVISION THE FUTURE
INTEGRATED

⊖ DIFFICULT TO CREATE
DIFFICULT TO MAINTAIN

gic level of value, differentiating you from your competitors and helping your competitors' clients identify new opportunities.

Level 1: Product

The lowest and most fundamental level of value is the value in your product or your service. Because of this, many sales organizations and their salespeople enter into a sales conversation by talking about their products or services. They share the features and benefits their prospective client will receive by using their product. When they're really sophisticated, they share "advantages," all the things the client will be able to do because of the product's features.

Make no mistake, it is important that you have a good product. A great product is even better. However, it is even more important to know that a great salesperson with an acceptable product beats a poor salesperson with an excellent product. The challenge here is that there are so many good and acceptable products in competitive markets like yours that your product by itself isn't differentiated or compelling enough to motivate a potential client to change partners. This is both why and how you've been commoditized.

If all you do is provide a good product, you will find it extremely difficult to generate any real loyalty from your clients. If your competitor creates only Level 1 value, the value created by their product alone, the act of displacement starts by entering into a conversation with your prospective client from a higher level of value. You misunderstand consultative selling if you believe that your product is the highest level of value your client needs from you. Staying at Level 1 is a recipe for losing clients.

Level 2: Service

When we provide clients with our product, we also create the need for service and support. Products sometimes fail. Other times, results are difficult to deliver. Clients need help making the product work and obtaining the outcomes we sell.

Helping your client implement, use, and troubleshoot your product is a higher level of value. Always being available to help your clients fully capture the value of what you sell differentiates you from Level 1 providers. The experience of what it is like to work with you is Level 2 value. Are you easy to do business with? Can you align what you do with the needs of the people who are going to interact with you and your business on a regular basis? Can you quickly and effectively solve the problems that come with buying and using your product?

Level 2 is greater than Level 1. If your competitor is creating only Level 1 value, they are creating an opening for you to displace them. If their service and delivery failures are not being promptly and properly addressed, this higher level of value can create a compelling reason to change. The costs of dealing with product failures compel people and companies to change every day. This is why Level 2 is necessary; it allows you to solve product and service problems.

For our purposes here, this is still what we call "entering from the left," with Level 1 being on the far left, and Level 2 next to it on the right. Even though it may be enough to eject your low-value competitor from their seat at the table, we will begin our strategy for displacement at an even higher level.

Level 3: Business Results

If you are in B2B sales, you are likely trying to operate and sell at Level 3. This is the level where you produce tangible business results. It's not the

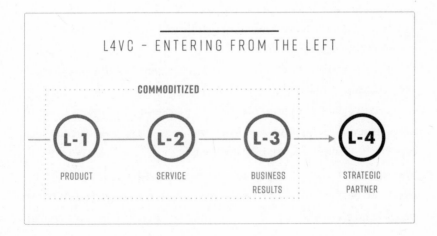

product alone that you sell. Nor is it the service and support. Instead, you sell the business improvement that your product or service produces for your client. You sell outcomes!

Maybe what you sell helps your client generate additional revenue. Or it might help make them more profitable by reducing their costs (which, to be clear, is not the same as lowering your price or helping them underinvest). You probably even have charts and spreadsheets that show how you can produce measurable results. This is a much higher level of value than either Level 1 or Level 2. Starting here is often enough to create a compelling case for change when you are competing against those sellers who sell at Levels 1 and 2. While that's all well and good, in B2B sales your serious competition will be with salespeople and sales organizations who also sell at Level 3. Almost every one of your serious competitors is trying to create Level 3 value.

This is now the highest level of commoditization. That means that while you have a spreadsheet that quantifies the value you create and your client's return on investment, your competitor has a spreadsheet that looks an awful lot like yours. And your client's purchasing department has a spreadsheet of their own that allows them to drop your prices into a couple cells and determine who has the lowest price (and on the rarest of rare occasions, a cell that determines lowest overall cost, many in purchasing being mostly unaware of or deliberately indifferent to the difference between price and cost*).

When all things are equal, your dream client is right to make their decision on price. If there is nothing better available, they have no compel-

---

* The price is what you charge for what you sell. The real cost is a measurement of the value created in an exchange. You can have the lowest price while also imposing a higher cost. For example, your lower price may come with higher errors, more returns, lower results, and additional costs that are incurred by your inefficiencies. Let's say you buy a pair of shoes with a price tag of $299 that last a full year. Another pair of shoes may have a price of $399 and last two years. You save $199 by buying the shoes with the higher price, because they last an additional year.

ling reason to change. If your product being better isn't enough to compel your dream clients to change, we must eliminate that as the starting point for executing a competitive displacement. If the experience, services, and support you offer won't move them to consider changing, then that too must be removed from the choices available to you. And if almost everyone can play the game at Level 3, then we are all swimming in the same red ocean, with little differentiation, all fighting for the same opportunities, all being perceived as commodities.

That means what has to be different isn't found in any of the three preceding levels. Scary, huh? You can't rely on your product to do the work, being so good and so compelling as to sell itself. Unless there was a line of people waiting to buy your product from you this morning, your product isn't likely to be enough to cause people to change. No matter how easy you are to do business with, your service and support isn't likely to be so different as to compel a change in partners. At least not by itself. And if everyone—or almost everyone—can play the game at Level 3, then that is off the table as a compelling differentiator.

The implications here are enormous for those of us who swim in red oceans. It means that there is only one place to turn to in order to find real differentiation, a competitive advantage, and a reason to change. Now, like it or not, *you* are the largest part of the value proposition. If you are going to live in a red ocean, you want the largest fins and biggest teeth. You want to be the great white shark.

Level 4: Strategic Partner

In *The Lost Art of Closing*, I wrote that you need only two things to be a trusted adviser: trust and advice. Being consultative requires that you give good counsel, the prerequisite being the business acumen and experience to be able to do so.

On the continuum of value creation, we put Level 1 value on the left

end, and the farthest point at the other end is Level 4, strategic partner. This is what we mean when we say, "Enter the conversation from the right." It means that we start with the highest level of value.

Levels 1 through 3 are not advice. The features and benefits of a product won't help you understand why you can no longer generate the results you need in a world of constant, accelerating, disruptive change. The services and support that create the experience of being easy to do business with don't help you achieve your longer-term strategic goals and outcomes. The fact that you produce tangible business results, while being critically important, doesn't help me understand what I need to do to deal with a future that will require me to make changes I haven't yet considered. A long-term strategic partnership now requires someone who can occupy the role of trusted adviser and offer good counsel. This requires playing at Level 4.

Level 4 means that you have the business acumen and situational knowledge (in other words, the experience) that allow you to create a strategic level of value. It means you understand and can explain the dissonance your dream client is experiencing; you can explain why they are struggling to produce the results they need and are challenged by their

LEVEL FOUR VALUE CREATION

STRATEGIC PARTNER 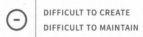 L-4

(+) STRATEGIC OUTCOMES
ENVISION & CREATE THE FUTURE
INTEGRATED
SOLVES TANGIBLE BUSINESS PROBLEMS
OUTSTANDING SERVICE & SUPPORT
GOOD PRODUCT OR SERVICE

(−) DIFFICULT TO CREATE
DIFFICULT TO MAINTAIN

current circumstances. You can explain to the client why and how they need to change before they need to make that change. This is the "advice" part of "trusted adviser."

DISPLACEMENT REQUIRES STRATEGIC VALUE + RELATIONSHIPS

To remove your competitor from your dream client's account, you need to create value that is strategic. This is the kind of value that provides them with a competitive advantage. It's built on insight and ideas. It's made up of your ability to help guide their business to a better future state. It also requires the ability to develop the relationships necessary to make change inside their company.

For our purposes here, we will use this operating philosophy: All things being equal, relationships win. All things being unequal, relationships still win. Your job is to make all things unequal by creating greater value by creating trusted relationships, the kind that allow you to deliver your advice—and have that advice taken. Let me explain.

If your offering and your competitor's offering are the same, then the person with the best relationship wins, there being no other real differentiation. If your competitor's offer is better, but you have deep relationships, you are still likely to win (we humans are not rational creatures, we are rationalizing creatures). When you sell, you do so with the intention of creating a preference to work with you, and that means creating more strategic outcomes and creating deeper working relationships.

You can ignore any advice that suggests that relationships are no longer necessary to selling effectively. They are even more important now, but they also require more of you now, namely your ability to create a higher level of value.

In the next chapter, we will develop the insights and ideas that allow you to create relationships of value. Before we do, we need to cover a little more ground here.

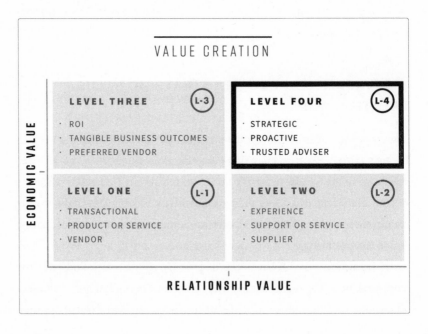

LEVELS STACK VALUE

I don't want you to walk away from this chapter with the belief that it isn't important to have a good product. It is important that your product, your service, or your solution works. There is no way you can be a strategic partner and a trusted adviser without having the ability to deliver something that works. Imagine having a terrible product and excellent service. You would not keep your clients very long if what you sell didn't do what it is supposed to do. That said, it may not have to be the very best product if your overall approach creates greater value. Your excellent service and support is additive. The local Starbucks I frequent knows me by name, and they know my order. This is something they work to be able to do as a way to create experience-level value, and it is impressive. It's also part of the reason they can sell coffee at higher margins than their competitors. No matter how well they know me, if their coffee was terrible, I would go elsewhere. If the coffee was great and the experience was terrible, I'd also go somewhere else (but not to Tim Hortons, their coffee not being nearly strong enough for my taste).

Level 3 is economic value. It's the return you provide for your client's investment in your product. You have a product that works, service and support that work, and the way you combine things creates a necessary return on investment. This level includes the prior levels. You don't have a solution that doesn't contain both your product and your experience.

At Level 4, strategic partner, you still need to create the other three levels of value. But in a sales conversation, there is a crucial difference between arriving at Level 4 value from the left by trying to add strategic value on top of your product features, customer experience, and economic value, and entering from the right by starting with strategic value. If you enter from Level 1 with the hopes of growing into Level 4, and open the conversation with your company, your product, and its features and benefits, you've established yourself as someone who offers nothing more than a product pitch. It is easier and more effective to establish yourself as a Level 4 value provider right from the start than to start at Level 1 and then redefine who you are and what you offer. By selling what you sell as a commodity, you are defined and treated accordingly (which likely means you find your way to the purchasing department, where commodities go to have their prices reduced and their margins shredded).

Executing a competitive displacement isn't easy, and it requires that you create value at different levels for different stakeholders. In later chapters, we will take a deep dive into understanding the different stakeholders, but for now you need to know that different groups of stakeholders generally need different value.

DIFFERENT STAKEHOLDERS NEED DIFFERENT LEVELS OF VALUE

You need to create all levels of value, as end users require Level 1, end users and ancillary stakeholders require Level 2, management and leadership require Level 3, and leadership requires Level 4.

The end user of your product needs it to work well for them. You will have a terrible time convincing the people who are going to use your product that they need to change if what you sell doesn't work. Level 1 value matters a great deal, and creating a preference to work with you means that end users need what you sell to work for them, even if it works only as well as what they have now. The strategic reason to change partners will not be compelling if you can't take care of the end users of your product.

There are other groups that need you to create Level 2 value. The end users need you to be easy to do business with, but so do the ancillary stakeholders, those people inside your dream client's company who don't use your product but will be affected by a decision to do so. This might be the accounting and finance groups who process your invoices and generate purchase orders or the information technology department (IT) who needs your solution to meet their technical standards. It could be engineering, who need compliance within a certain boundary of acceptable technical specifications. The point here is that you need to be "easy to do business with." You need good service and good support, and you need to take care of the stakeholders in other departments, beyond the end users.

The management team, purchasing department, and executive leadership all need you to create a return on the investment they are making in your product or service. They need you to create Level 3 value. You need to be able to show them what value they get for their investment in your product. This is the level of value most sales organizations create now.

But Level 4 does more. Level 4 provides the reason to do something different in the first place. Level 4 provides the compelling reason to change, a vision of a better future, and a strategic view of your prospective client's business. This level serves executive leadership. It's strategic, and that trumps the lower levels of value.

SUPER TRANSACTIONAL OR SUPER RELATIONAL

The concept of levels of value describes the way markets are being pulled in two different directions. Where no real value creation is necessary, where what is being purchased is a true commodity, prices are being reduced to the lowest point possible. Companies are competing by being super transactional, removing the friction of buying and lowering costs. This is the strategy of Level 1 and Level 2 value providers. It is important to note that when a company makes this decision, it is a strategic decision. Super transactional does not simply mean discounting or making pricing concessions. This is how these companies consistently compete.

The opposite strategy is super relational. This is high trust, high value, high caring. This approach is the very opposite of super transactional, placing greater value on providing results, being proactive, developing customer intimacy, and having deep knowledge and expertise. When decisions are complex, with many factors at play and many possible paths forward, relationships of value matter a great deal. This is the strategy of Levels 3 and 4, and because most B2B sales organizations have been creating Level 3, selling the tangible return on investment and solving their client's existing problems to the point of it being a commodity, success in creating opportunities and acquiring and retaining clients requires Level 4. Level 4 is disruptive in that it allows you to compel change.

If you behave like you are super transactional, intentionally or unintentionally, you will be treated like a commodity. You will be an attractive alternative only to prospects who care mostly about price, even if they do so to their detriment. This is to be a vendor or supplier (two words that you should be horrified to ever hear your client utter when referring to you), not a trusted adviser (words that produce the sweetest sound to your ears).

Alternatively, if you are super relational, you will attract companies and people who want better results. You will be interesting to people who are growth oriented and people who want to address their systemic challenges and threats and move their companies forward. Being super relational is what makes you a trusted adviser.

THE DISINTERMEDIATION OF SALESPEOPLE

We cannot leave this chapter without addressing the fact that the inability to create a higher level of value is the root cause of the disintermediation of salespeople. If you believe that your product should sell itself, then you are an order-taker, and the future doesn't need order-takers; technological solutions are already eliminating roles where no value is created by an interaction with a salesperson. Right now, you are likely to have an app on your phone that serves as the salesperson for many things you buy. Even you, a salesperson, buy without a salesperson (and you may come home to a stack of packages on your front porch, none of which required more than just a click, a daily occurrence at Casa de Iannarino).

If you believe that being able to produce a tangible result will allow you to succeed in sales, you are likely focused on responding to identified opportunities, and not the real work of being a salesperson and trusted adviser, which is creating opportunities.

There is no reason for a client to change partners unless there is an advantage to be gained by doing so. If you cannot create greater value than your dream client's current partner, you are not providing a reason to change. You need to be the person who can create new opportunities that are worth pursuing, by providing a vision of a better future and compelling change. You also need to be the person who brings that change to life.

From this point forward, you will enter the conversation from the right, a higher, more strategic, and more complete approach to value creation, and one that is now necessary.

Now that you know what Level 4 value is, we can move on to using it to capture mindshare, the next step on our way to displacing your competitors.

DO THIS NOW

1. Make a list of five contacts in your top five dream clients. What level of value would they say you create for them? Write down your best guess for each of them (Level 1, 2, 3, or 4).

2. Write down three things that you might do to move up to a higher level of value for each of these prospective client contacts.

   To download the worksheet that accompanies this chapter, go to www.eattheirlunch.training.

Chapter 2

CAPTURING MINDSHARE

IN THIS CHAPTER, WE'LL LOOK AT HOW TO DEVELOP THE IDEAS that you need to execute the approach in the prior chapter. I do not pretend that any of this is easy, or that it is only a one-time effort. The work of identifying ideas that matter and shaping an opinion as to what your dream client needs to do now to ensure their success in the future is something you have to do continually, forever. In a world of constant, accelerating, disruptive change, you must continually adjust.

THE BATTLE FOR MINDSHARE

One of the most underappreciated metrics in sales is wallet share, the percentage that is indicated by what portion of the client's total spend they are spending with you. I have never understood why some salespeople and sales organizations go to all the trouble to win a new opportunity and then settle for 10 percent of the company's spending in their category without so much as a fight. Even when they have the contract and contacts, many salespeople spend their efforts on winning new clients, never doing the work that would improve their clients' results and win more of their business as a result. They do nothing—or very little—to grow the business they've already won.

But there is a metric that's much harder to quantify and much more important than wallet share because it precedes wallet share. In fact, it's the biggest part of what allows for the command of wallet share, and it's what is essential to eating your competitor's lunch. This metric is subjective, but the result is quite tangible. That metric is mindshare.

Mindshare means that you own a portion of your prospective client's thinking. It means that you have shaped their thinking by sharing insights and ideas with them as it pertains to the areas where you are a subject matter expert. Mindshare is the lens through which the client looks at their business, their challenges, and their opportunities. You are providing the lens that shapes what your dream client sees and how they see it, and you are trying to replace the lens that your competitor already has in place. This is a noisy world where there are so many voices, particularly on social media, many of whom don't know beans from Brussels sprouts, providing information and ideas without any real experience or insight (and in many cases sharing such compelling content as cute cat videos, their personal politics, and their current fitness routines). Social media is a powerful medium, but only if used with the intention of shaping mindshare.

Displacing your competitor starts by developing mindshare. You start by changing the lens through which your dream client views their business, and by doing so create a compelling case to do something different. Right now, I'm creating mindshare with you: you've just discovered that there are four levels of value. In sharing that with you, I have now infected you with the idea that you are creating too little value for some of your clients, and you start to recognize a gap between the way you approach clients now and a better way to start those conversations. I have offered you a lens that provides you with the value of a clearer, crisper view of what you need to do to take customers from your competitors.

By changing the lens through which your dream client sees their business, you become known as the person who understands the changes occurring now, what they mean for your clients, and what they should be doing about it. In other words, you must create a reputation for yourself as someone who can create a super-relational level of value, which means you create economic and strategic value while also being the person your dream client wants on their team.

The difference in the value you create and the value your competitor creates begins with the development of business acumen and situational awareness. You need to develop a line of thinking around the trends that will eventually cause your competitor's client to change, and you must help them decide to change before they are forced to by some negative event, or before they miss an opportunity.

How do you develop this thinking and produce valuable insights? You want to start with newspapers, whether printed, digital, or both. You need to stay up-to-date on economic, political, legal, technological, scientific, and cultural trends, since all of these affect your client in some way, and you can mine them for insights, things that will impact your dream clients. Magazines and business journals also work to help you with ideas and insights, as do the publications that are specific to your industry or your client's industry.

You can also watch or listen to business shows on channels like CNBC, where you will hear business leaders and analysts discuss businesses, their strategies, and their results. You can learn a lot by listening to how CEOs think about their business and their strategies. I picked up one of my favorite stories from watching an interview with Reed Hastings, the CEO of Netflix, when the company first started gaining national attention. When the reporter challenged his business model, noting that he was sending DVDs by mail and at risk of losing to someone who delivered videos over the Internet, Hastings expressed his awareness of that fact, shooting back, "That's why we named the company Netflix and not DVDs by mail." That interview makes clear that Hastings had a view of where technology and entertainment were heading long before most people.

That said, you should start with written content, not television or radio, because later you'll want to collect these articles as proof of your insights. When you identify trends and ideas that matter, keep a file so you can use them to help shape the lens through which your dream client thinks about the future of their business.

I want to be very clear about what you take away from this. If you want to be a trusted adviser, it is your responsibility to develop your ability to deliver advice. No one is going to do this for you. You have to educate yourself if you intend to educate your clients. This is never truer than when you are asking your dream client to replace their existing partner.

DISSONANCE AND THE STATUS QUO

Your clients have challenges understanding their environment and producing the results they need. They're not sure why they can no longer produce the results they need, and they desperately want things to "go back to normal," to a time when what they are doing worked. Even when they are currently in a strong position, you create value for them by helping them anticipate and prepare for coming challenges in a way that allows them to extend or improve their performance. Most of your dream clients are deeply entrenched in the status quo and are committed to staying the course. As challenges arise, they resort to short-term workarounds and hacks that allow them to postpone more substantial change for longer than they should. Change is scary, but it's infinitely scarier if you don't have the confidence to know what you need to change and how.

This marks the change in sales from what worked in the past to what works now. In the past, your clients understood their world better than they do now. They were more certain about what needed to change and what actions to take. Eliciting these things was enough to create an opportunity.

They would have also had an easier time putting something new in place, there being far fewer people involved in a decision to change.

Contrast that with today, when your clients are faced with a world that no longer makes sense and is more uncertain than ever. A world in which whole industries are being reimagined. One where upstarts with new business models are destroying old ones. There is greater pressure to improve financial results while using fewer resources. Meanwhile, more people in the client organization are being held responsible for the company's financial performance. Because the world we now occupy is one of constant, accelerating, disruptive change, we are less sure about what we should do—and even more challenged getting consensus around the definition of the problem and the solution.

Here's a short list of a few of the forces making things more uncertain:

- Technological changes fueled by the Internet, the Internet of Things, and the ubiquity of handheld devices has reshaped businesses, business models, and customer expectations.
- Globalization has brought greater competition, lower wages, and downward pressure on margins and a drive for greater financial results.
- Populist movements throughout the Western world are reshaping politics in stable countries.
- Whole industries are being disintermediated by technologies that didn't exist a few years ago.
- Government spending is rising, as are the burdens of aging populations and the expenses of their health care, all of which create a larger tax burden on companies.

Think of the impact these things have had on your life. You are likely to book your flight on an app, travel to work in an Uber (or an electric car), drive through Starbucks to pick up the coffee you ordered on an app, read the news on your iPad, and stay at an Airbnb while on your work trip. Your company may have a work-from-home policy, require that all communication is done over an app like Slack or Microsoft Teams instead of email, and hold meetings using a video web-conferencing solution. Depending on your age, there is a substantial chance that you met your significant other online. As retired army general Eric Shinseki put it, "If you don't like change, you're going to like irrelevance even less."

The speed of change today and uncertainty about the future are at the root of the dissonance your clients experience. There is a disharmonious clashing of your clients' beliefs and the reality in which they find themselves.

Enter the trusted adviser. The trusted adviser makes sense of the world in which her clients find themselves. She understands the forces that are at work on her client's business and has a command of the facts. She can see into the future with greater clarity and knows what needs to be done now, how it needs to be done, and how to help make the necessary changes. This starts with the ability to explain the dissonance, making certain what is uncertain. She is confident and direct about what decisions need to be made and what actions must be taken.

There are two major reasons why you must occupy this space. First, if there is information parity and your client knows as much as or more than you do about what they should be doing as it pertains to what you sell, you are unnecessary. We are back to trust and advice. If I don't need your advice or count on you to do my thinking for me in some area, then you cannot be my trusted adviser. You are at best redundant, and at worst an annoyance, wasting my time with Level 1 conversations (as short as they are when you bring no real value).

Second, and equally important, if your competitor knew what you know now and shared your beliefs about what needs to change, they'd already have moved your dream client forward to that better future. If they do know what the client should be doing but haven't been able to get them to execute the necessary changes, they don't have the mindshare they need—or they don't have it at the right level.

The Chinese character for the word "crisis" is made up of two characters, one that means danger and a second that can be interpreted as opportunity. In a world of constant, accelerating, disruptive change, your role is to identify the opportunities while helping your dream client avoid the dangers.

THE IMPACT OF SUPER TRENDS

There are large, universal trends that explain the dissonance your clients experience. These are tectonic shifts, like demographic, technological, political, and economic changes. These super trends provide opportunities and challenges, both of which lead to change.

The reason we look for super trends when it comes to making the case for change is because they are so valuable in explaining the dissonance a client is experiencing and because they are irrefutable. The facts about super trends are so well documented, studied, and validated that they are impossibly difficult to argue with or ignore. This shifts any argument from a disagreement about what is happening to discussing what it means, and that is the exact conversation you need to start to begin displacing your competitor by establishing yourself as a trusted adviser.

How does this work? Let's take the example of one current super trend. At the time of this writing, late 2017, there are presently eleven thousand baby boomers retiring every day in the United States. This is 4.3 million people each year. This means that their jobs will need to be refilled. It also means that they will be eligible for government-subsidized health care and Social Security. Many of them will have incomes that are greatly reduced.

These are facts that are not in dispute. They are useful in setting up the case for change, but facts alone don't tell me what any of this means. I need insight, understanding. I need to know how this affects my business.

With 4.3 million people retiring, you'll need a strategy to replace those employees with people who both want and need those jobs. For employment levels to stay even requires that 358,000 people backfill the open positions each month, and this assumes that younger generations want those jobs and have the necessary skills. Later generations may not find certain jobs desirable and may prefer to work in the "gig economy," deciding to freelance instead of working in a cubicle. It also means that the employees you need may not share the same values, preferring a different environment (one in which a young man can wear a beard that wouldn't look out of place on a lumberjack and a man bun that looks like something out of an Akira Kurosawa samurai movie). The question here is, "What should your talent acquisition strategy be as the workforce undergoes a massive generational shift?"

With so many boomers retiring and living longer (another indisputable fact), government spending on health care is certain to rise due to the sheer number of people who will be covered. This means that government will spend more money, and more mandates on business are likely. The costs of doing business will rise over time. The question here is, "What should you be doing now to factor in the certain-to-increase costs of doing business?"

This is one super trend and two questions. Notice that the questions I asked at the end of each of the preceding paragraphs have no easy answer. There are lots of decisions that might be made, and there can be wildly different strategies for different businesses based on their position, their strategy, and their resources. Opinions here will vary, and necessarily so. The reason we are asking these questions is so that we can explain the dissonance ("Why are we having so much trouble finding the people we need now?") while also causing our prospective client to discover something about themselves, namely that they haven't thought this through well enough to know what they should be doing or how they should react.

We are also setting up a conversation where we get to apply our ideas, our business acumen, and our situational knowledge. We get to provide our advice based on our view and our experience. Maybe the right way to deal with the challenge of finding talent is to replace some roles with technology, automating some positions. Another choice might be outsourcing functions to another company that specializes in producing some result, eliminating the need for the role altogether. The right choice could be to create a new value proposition that appeals to the talent you need. Maybe the right answer is some combination of all of the above.

The answer to the challenge of rising costs based on major changes in government mandates and taxes may be to raise prices to accommodate these new costs. Or it might also be to reduce other internal costs to ensure your profitability. It might require that you change your pricing altogether, using some kind of cost-plus model, one in which you mark up the costs of doing business to allow for these fluctuations by passing them on to your clients to ensure that you continue to run a profitable business. Opinions here can vary, and the right answer will be different for different companies at different times. So how do you demonstrate you have the chops to provide advice, and how do you know what advice to offer?

There are two factors that demonstrate that you have the required expertise to offer good advice. The first is that you have a command of the facts and what they mean. So far, that is what we have been covering in this chapter on mindshare. Deciding what advice to give is more complicated, being made up of your situational knowledge. This is the second factor, and equally critical to capturing mindshare. This is your experience in seeing the different decisions people make and their outcomes. The advice you provide needs to be based on your knowledge and experience, and your understanding of the client's situational context. It's worth noting that your experience can be greatly increased by capturing the knowledge and experience of all the people in your company who are working to help clients produce better results.

Your knowledge and advice are what make you a trusted adviser and what allow you to steal mindshare.

TECHNOLOGICAL, POLITICAL, ECONOMIC, SCIENTIFIC, AND CULTURAL TRENDS

Perhaps the best way to show you how you capture mindshare and create a compelling case for change is to demonstrate it here. To do so, let's look at a couple industries to identify relevant trends and what they mean. These will serve as a model as you develop your own talk tracks. Being able to show evidence and relate anecdotes about these trends can help you create and justify the need to change now.

Example 1: Selling Financial Services

Here is an example of how you might enter the conversation from Level 4 if you sold financial services. Here we'll look at the trends, their implications, and what might be a view or a set of values that compels change.

Trends:

- Human life expectancy is projected to grow.
  - A woman in the United States will live to be 83.3 and a man will live to be 79.3 years old.
- Inflation rates are expected to rise.
  - Inflation has risen from 1.6 to 2.2 percent over the last year and is trending up.

- Health care costs are increasing.
  - Health care costs were $27.2 billion in 1960, or 5 percent of GDP. This amounted to $146 per person.
  - Health care costs were $3.3 trillion in 2016, or 17.9 percent of GDP. This amounts to $10,348 per person.
- Personal savings rates are declining.
  - In 1960, the personal savings rate was 10.6 percent.
  - In 2018 that rate is 3.4 percent.
- Government spending on health care will reach $5.7 trillion by 2025 and grow faster than GDP.
  - Government spending on health care has grown by 4.2 percent annually between 2008 and 2016.

Life expectancy is mostly the result of scientific advancements (with a big part being attributed to fewer people smoking). Inflation is an economic trend. Health care costs are driven by economic trends as well as governmental and political factors. The savings rate is a cultural trend; the drop-off may be largely due to the mind-set of people who were born during the Great Depression and World War II never experiencing anything so painful. They saved more to hedge against another serious downturn. Later generations don't always share those fears.

All of these trends are facts that build a case for why your customer needs to change now. But to help them recognize the need to change, you need to have a point of view about what these facts mean and a strong opinion about what your dream client needs to do to address them. There are implications, negative consequences, for maintaining the status quo. There are also positive outcomes for taking action now to address these trends.

You might start this conversation with a slide on each one of these trends, opening the conversation by saying, "There are five trends that are causing our clients to change and make some of the decisions we are recommending. The facts show that we are living longer, that inflation is growing, health care costs are increasing, personal savings rates are at all-time lows, and government spending is increasing."

Implications:

- You will live longer than you might believe.
- Inflation will cause the money you save to be worth less in the future.
- Health care costs are increasing, meaning more of your money will be spent on this category in the future.
- Most people aren't saving enough to account for inflation or increasing health care costs.
- Government spending on health care will increase but will force choices about reducing coverage or requiring the recipient to pay more.

You can weave the facts into a case for change by exploring the implications: "We are going to live longer than we might have believed, the money we save will be negatively impacted by inflation, we'll need more money for health care in the future, and the government will be as cash-strapped as we are."

And with this we are back to the advice part of being a trusted adviser. You've shared what is going on in your prospective client's world, you've explained what it means, and now you need to share what you believe your prospective client needs to do now.

Advice:

- You'll need to save and invest a lot more money than you might believe.
- You'll need to choose vehicles that allow you to reach your goals.

• You'll need to make adjustments more frequently than you have in the past.

How you offer your advice matters a great deal. You need to compel your client to change, but you don't want to overplay your hand and create resistance. You might say, "Some of the things we are recommending now include saving and investing a little more, choosing better vehicles to protect those investments from inflation, and making more frequent adjustments to their plans."

There is fairly universal advice, providing you with some reasonable assumptions to make about a very common problem your prospective clients are facing, known or unknown. However, the advice you give may change from one prospective client to the next.

In the past, you might have shown up as a Level 1 salesperson, presenting your investment offerings and describing their features and benefits. You might have leaned heavily on your company's history and longevity as proof that you are credible and someone who is worth doing business with. You may even have done an analysis to prove that your prospect isn't well prepared for their future. If that is your approach, it explains why you are struggling to displace your competitor; you are not trading value, you are not helping them understand why they have to change, and you are not capturing mindshare. You are not compelling change.

In this example, you have shown up as Level 4. You have entered the conversation with a discussion of strategic outcomes instead of the tired trope of describing your company and your products and services. By starting the conversation about your prospective client's world and what changes are necessary, you very naturally lead to the conversation about solutions, the "what do we do about this and how do we do it?"

Example 2: Selling Technology

For this example, we'll look at the trends that will cause people who buy technology to change. Think of companies that sell software as a service (SaaS) or companies that sell something like enterprise resource planning.

Trends:

- Cloud computing eliminates operational issues and reduces costs.
  - Companies are eliminating non–core competencies, including running servers, and are scaling their software to meet the needs of their business.
  - They are also pursuing speed to results.
- More employees are working from home.
  - In 2016, 45 percent of employees said they sometimes work from home.
- Technological progress is experiencing exponential growth, and consumers are adopting new technology faster.
  - Advancements in technology are also enabling companies to better serve their clients.
- Consumers have higher expectations of the companies with which they do business.
  - Consumers expect greater responsiveness, personalization, and access to their information.
  - They promote companies that are responsive to their needs and punish others.

These trends are technological and cultural. We could very easily add the time and challenges of updating software hosted on-site, the integration of artificial intelligence, machine learning, processing power, or the cost of hiring employees with the technical expertise to run a non-core part of the business versus outsourcing.

You might start this conversation by saying, "The four trends that we believe are going to have the biggest impact on your business over the next eighteen to twenty-four months are (1) the growing ability of companies to outsource non–core competencies through cloud computing and the resulting cost savings, (2) the increasing speed with which people adopt new technologies, (3) providing access critical to your success in equipping your workforce, and (4) meeting your customer's new expectations."

Implications:

- Companies that devote time and energy to non–core competencies spend more time and money to produce results that would be gained faster and at less expense by choosing to outsource certain functions.
- Because more people are working from home, new technologies need to be adopted to allow them to gain access to resources, to communicate, and to collaborate when they are away from the office (if they even have one).
- Both employees and customers expect that their companies will provide them with the technologies they need to interact with the company.
- Customers expect to be able to connect with and contact the companies they do business with over multiple channels, and they punish those that respond slowly.

The conversation you have with your client might go like this: "Companies that outsource non–core competencies free up money to invest in the core competencies that create a competitive advantage." This language reshapes what would have been a product pitch into a conversation about the strategic advantage it enables.

Having had this conversation, we can now share our views and our values as we provide advice to our prospective client.

Advice:

- Adopt cloud-based, SaaS solutions to reduce your overall costs by reducing your spend on expensive IT resources while providing an upgraded experience for your clients and employees. Invest the savings in your core competencies, where you create value for your clients or customers.
- Enable a work-from-home and remote workforce by providing the tools that allow them to connect and collaborate across distance while giving them an experience that is as good as or better than what they would have were they located in an office.
- Because your customers demand access to their data, reporting, and the ability to request support and changes, provide them with solutions that give multichannel support and access to better serve them.

The advice you provide here should be equally strategic: "We believe that you should eliminate your non-core technology to reduce your expenses and invest the savings in acquiring new clients." I want you to notice something about the advice you are offering here: it holds true whether your dream client chooses you or someone else. This is your point of view about what your dream client should do. But by teaching your client to understand their world and providing your ideas to improve their business, you establish trust and make the case for why they should partner with you.

This is a Level 4 approach. We started with facts about what is going on in the world, we shared what it means to the client, and then we shared our views and values, what we believe to be the right choices here. To make these examples useful, I chose broad trends to tell these two stories, so you could get a view of the mechanics of selling in a way that gives you a competitive advantage.

How does this relate to our primary goal of displacing your competitor inside your dream client's account? When you show up at Level 1, 2, or 3, you are covering ground that your competitor is already covering. They already provide a product or service that, while maybe not as good as what you have to offer, is good enough. Either your competitor is providing a good experience, or your dream client has learned to live with their shortcomings, in which case compelling change by being easy to do business with might work for a few stakeholders; it is less likely to compel the C-suite to change. They're also getting some sort of result that is good enough (even though you know it isn't good enough and the status quo may be putting your dream client at greater risk).

DEVELOPING A THEME

Without an understanding of the trends that are going to impact your dream client's business, and without some idea as to how they should respond to those trends, you can't sell at Level 4. It's your understanding and your ability to guide your dream clients forward through your insights and ideas and experience that define you.

Imagine two salespeople, one who has the talk tracks outlined above, and the other who is deprived of them. The first salesperson can explain what's going on in the world, why things are now more difficult, and what to do about it. This salesperson starts the conversation with these talk tracks instead of their solution. The second salesperson shows up and shares what amounts to a product listing that provides less detailed information than their website (a conversation that is unlikely to last more than a few minutes).

Taking the first salesperson's approach allows you to come in at Level 4 and position yourself as a trusted adviser who can compel change. It allows you to recommend decisions that are strategic, outcomes that your product, service, and solutions will help your dream client achieve. There is no need to remove your competitor if there isn't a greater outcome to be gained by doing so. If your product, service, and solution is similar to your competitor's, moving up to a higher level of value is where you are going to identify the compelling reason to change. Your product, service, or solution is only interesting as a response to the reasons your dream client needs to change to meet their strategic needs. This is why it creates an opportunity for a displacement. You have now flanked your competitor, pushed a new lens in front of their client, and established yourself as the person who can move them forward. Your competitor is now on the defense. Your competitor also has the heavy burden of what we might call "the curse of the incumbent." When your dream client has known their partner for years—or decades—without their having to prove that they provide strategic value, it's more difficult for them to establish themselves as strategic partners now. Their client believes they've already seen the best they have to offer. And they probably have.

Finally, you need a unifying theme to present your ideas to your dream clients. You need a statement, a big idea that describes the changes that have occurred or are occurring now. This theme is what you will use to provide a structure to your insights, your ideas, and your big questions.

If I had to identify a theme running through all my books so far, I might tie them all together under the theme of "Becoming a Trusted Adviser in a World of Constant, Accelerating, Disruptive Change." You might take the trends around baby boomers retiring and develop a theme called "The Coming Increase in Social Safety Net Spending and Its Impact on Small Business." Using the two examples here, the themes might be "Ensuring the Quality of Your Life on the Back Nine," or "Shifting Your

Investments to More Strategic Outcomes." What you want here is some overarching theme that captures the trend and its impact. This is your point of view. This is how you capture mindshare.

The person who can create the case for change is the person your dream client is most likely to choose as a partner. This is mindshare, and you develop it only when you have information disparity, when you know things your dream client doesn't know now.

DO THIS NOW

1. Identify four or five trends that will cause your dream client to change now or in the future.

2. Write down the questions these trends should be causing the client to consider now.

3. Make a list of the changes the client should be making now to address the changes in their industry or market.

   To download the worksheet that accompanies this chapter, go to www.eattheirlunch.training.

Chapter 3

CREATING AN OPENING THROUGH NURTURE CAMPAIGNS AND PURSUIT PLANS

TO DEVELOP THE RELATIONSHIPS THAT ALLOW YOU TO CREATE an opportunity and displace your competitor, you need a plan to nurture those relationships over a long period of time. You need a strategy to establish yourself as someone who can create a different level of value. You need to share ideas consistently, and professionally persist in pursuing meetings with your competitor's clients.

In this chapter, we'll build out that plan to nurture your dream clients over time, using different messages, different cadences, and different media, always establishing you as the person who can make a difference. Your pursuit plan will distinguish you as someone who knows what needs to change, why it needs to change, and how to make those changes. While your competitor is resting on their laurels, confident that they are at no great risk of losing their client, you are positioning yourself as that client's next partner. While it's business as usual for your competitor, you are doing the heavy lifting of capturing mindshare and making the case that things need to change, that they can be better.

HOW TO INTRODUCE YOURSELF TO YOUR DREAM CLIENT

It very much matters how you enter into a conversation with your dream client. It is important that you start as a trusted adviser type, as a professional, and as a peer. You have to embody this role from the very first communication. This means that you must have something to say that your dream client believes is worth their time to discover. You can't enter into the conversation with a self-oriented approach, and some of the older ways are now off limits because they don't achieve the outcome you need here.

This is a very traditional way to ask for a meeting. It still works, even if it works against your goals.

"Hi. This is Anthony Iannarino, and I am with XYZ Widgets, the leading manufacturer of widgets. I'd like to stop by and introduce myself and my company and learn a little bit about you and your company. Does Tuesday at one p.m. work or is Wednesday at ten a.m. better?"

There is a lot here to unpack. First, by offering to introduce yourself and your services, you have projected that this meeting is about you. You have reminded your dream client why they don't like to take meetings with salespeople, suggesting that you're going to bring a slide deck about your company's storied history, your locations, your leadership team, and the logos of all the well-recognized companies that buy from your company. Naturally, you will want to ask a few questions before pitching your product.

Second, and adding insult to injury, you've decided to use a closing technique that is four or five decades old and one that projects a self-orientation and smarminess that repels clients. It's called the "alternative of choice" because it is supposed to eliminate the choice not to meet with you. Even if it works from time to time, there are better approaches available to you. Let's explore what it might look like to introduce yourself and enter into a conversation from a higher level of value, one where you immediately establish yourself as someone with the ideas and insights necessary to help people produce better results.

"Good morning. This is Anthony Iannarino with XYZ Widgets. I am calling you today to ask you for a twenty-minute meeting where I can share with you an executive briefing about four trends that will have the biggest impact on manufacturers in the next eighteen to twenty-four months. I'll also provide you with the questions we are answering for our clients, so you can share them with your management team there at AAA. How does Thursday look for a twenty-minute briefing?"

This is a different starting point. I am stating the fact that I know what the four biggest trends are and how they will affect my dream client's business. It also makes clear that I know what questions need to be asked and answered to deal with the challenges these trends present. I am even willing to provide these questions to my dream client, so she can share them with her management team, meaning she can start down this path without me if she so chooses. Most of all, I am trading value in excess of the time I am asking for. This imbalance is in my dream client's favor as they trade twenty minutes for insights that can change the results they are producing. Also notice that I did not promise to talk about me, my company, or my products. That would be to start at Level 1 instead of starting at Level 4. If you want to stake out the territory of Level 4, you start there.

YOU ARE GOING TO HEAR NO

Does my pitch for a meeting mean that you are never going to hear "no"? Absolutely not. Time being the single, finite, nonrenewable resource that it is, your dream clients will work like the devil to protect their time. Even if you get a no, you have still introduced yourself as someone who has ideas about what has to change, why it has to change, and how to make those changes. By leveraging the super trends we identified in the last chapter, you are well set up to start from Level 4.

Even more important, when your dream client already has a partner sitting in your seat, we aren't planning to make a call, walk in, and rip the business away from our competitor. That would not be a very thoughtful plan, nor would it be likely to succeed. Even though you will absolutely have contacts say yes to your meeting request, competitive displacements require that we play the long game, that we professionally persist over time, methodically developing the relationships and the case for change that creates an opportunity.

What's most important here is that your dream client hears your voice. You are establishing that you are someone who can help them understand why their current state is untenable and why they are struggling, as well as creating a vision of a better future state and the knowledge of how to get there.

You don't want to start this conversation over email. Email is the choice of salespeople who start at a lower level of value. They mistakenly believe that sending an email first warms up the prospective client for their phone call. It does nothing of the sort. No contact inside your prospective client's account receives an email and thinks to themselves, "How thoughtful of this salesperson to email me. I am going to remember their name. I hope they call me soon." Email is what you use to follow up a phone call or a voice mail message. You are not going to use email to ask for a meeting. You will use email to share ideas of value and let your contact know that you'll try them again later, it being your responsibility to call them back, not vice versa.

BUILDING THE CASE FOR CHANGE

There are four primary types of content you need to build the case for change and begin the process of displacing your competitor. These four different types of content combine to help shape mindshare and create an opportunity.

Why Change

There may be four trends that will change your dream client's current situation so much that they need to do something different to succeed now and in the future. There may be six trends, or just three really big and nasty trends that are going to harm their business (even if harm means missing opportunities). It doesn't matter how many trends as much as it matters that they help you make the case for change.

Let's stick with the trend that I riffed on in chapter 2, the one about eleven thousand baby boomers retiring every day in the United States. How do you use a trend like this to suggest that your prospective client needs to change?

First, let's look at this through a set of questions that are complicated, difficult to answer, and require real change:

- With the talent pool shrinking at this pace, what is your strategy to identify and compete for the employees you need to run your business?
- What are you going to do to create an employee value proposition that attracts the people you need?
- How does your value proposition speak to younger generations, the people who are coming into the workforce with different expectations?
- How do you intend to close the skills gap and the experience gap that are being created now by the baby boomers retiring?

Now let's transform these questions into "why change now." Let's make them declarative statements.

- The talent pool is shrinking and companies that want to succeed in the future will need to be more competitive about acquiring the employees they need, especially in skilled roles and leadership.
- What employees want is at odds with what most companies offer as their employee value proposition.
- Later generations want to work for companies where their work is flexible and where it provides purpose and meaning.
- Certain skills are in short supply and too few people have the experience they need to effectively take some roles.

This is how you begin the process of leveraging your ideas and insights to create a case for change. It is how you take what you learned in the first two chapters of this book and weaponize it, making it actionable.

By doing this, you are starting to create a gap between the value you and the client's current provider are bringing to the table. First, if your competitor were paying attention to these trends and ideas and recognized that they should be compelling change, they'd already be helping your dream client to do something to address them. If they are paying attention and sharing the ideas without the client changing, there may be some problem in the relationship that diminishes their credibility or prevents their client from acting on their advice. You are creating a gap and capturing mindshare by sharing your thinking here. Second, if your competitor is aware of these factors and is unable to make the case for change, they already have a problem that creates an opening for a competitive displacement.

The content that you share with your dream clients should speak to the reasons they need to change. It should explain the dissonance they are experiencing, providing an understanding of what is changing and why what they are used to doing is either no longer working—or soon won't be.

By establishing yourself as the person who knows what is changing, what it means for their company, what they need to change, and how to change it, you are positioning yourself to create an opportunity—and a competitive displacement.

This brings us to the primary change in what is required of salespeople and sales organizations today. In the past, you could assume that your dream client was already dissatisfied, and all you had to do was elicit their dissatisfaction to create an opportunity. Now it is your responsibility to create the case for change instead of waiting for an event to cause your dream client to raise their hand and ask for help. Waiting and responding is a lower level of value when it comes to commercial relationships. You cannot be a trusted adviser if your client has to fall behind so much that they've been hurt by not changing. A trusted adviser would do something before their client was harmed.

There is a small challenge in providing the "why change now" message. That challenge is that you are a salesperson, and you are eventually going to try to sell your client your product. Of course, you would say these things are true. That means your dream client is right to have a certain skepticism, a skepticism that you must address.

Providing Proof

If I tell you that 4.3 million baby boomers are retiring every year, or eleven thousand a day, you may or may not believe me. But when the Bureau of Labor Statistics says it's true, it's true. When the *Wall Street Journal* and the *New York Times* report it, it's a fact. Trusted third parties, people, and companies that stand to gain nothing by sharing these facts, make them true. It is your job to validate that what you are sharing as fact is indeed true. If you want to be a credible source, you need to cite your work. Stealing someone else's work makes you a plagiarist, but citing another person's work makes you a scholar and thought leader. You want to be the latter.

There are countless third-party sources you can use to provide proof of your statements. You can use government data, like the Bureau of Labor Statistics, census information, and other governmental economic reports. You can use third-party information about legislative changes and their impact on businesses. Research organizations like Forrester, Gartner, and Gallup produce information on trends and their impact, all of which provide confidence in their validity. Newspapers and magazines can also provide proof that the super trends you are describing are real and that they are going to impact your dream client's business.

What you are looking for here are articles and reports that validate the trends you are using to message "why change now." When you can stack multiple views on top of one another, the trends you have identified as being real threats and opportunities become true. Use good and solid evidence to support your argument.

Facts and Figures

If a picture is worth a thousand words, then a well-placed visual representation of data is worth ten thousand. There are some contacts within your dream client account who will believe what you are suggesting only when they see the data for themselves. We live in an age in which massive data is being created and captured and used to provide insights. These insights allow us to make better decisions. We have greater visibility into who we are, what we do, and what it means because we have this information. More and more, the decision makers you are pursuing will want to see the data for themselves. Some of them will also want some way of deriving the meaning for themselves.

Providing facts and figures helps you displace your competitor in two ways. First, it provides a different level of proof. In addition to third-party validation, it provides the facts themselves, unencumbered by your analysis. This is "see for yourself." Second, it requires your contact to start to decide what the data means to them. Without an analysis or interpretation that comes with other proof providers, your contact has to think about what they are seeing and what it means. This prevents it from being something theoretical and abstract and motivates your dream client to become emotionally invested in "why change now."

So far you've made the case for "why change now" and provided proof that these trends are real and need to be addressed. This third type of content, facts and figures, helps enable your dream client to make sense of what they are seeing for themselves. Which brings us to the fourth and final type of content you need to share to create an opportunity: your views and values, or how to change.

Views and Values

What does all this mean? What should I think about these trends, this proof, this data? How do I make sense of this and what should I be doing now? If you are going to be a trusted adviser, you need to have advice. You need to provide good counsel on what should be done, when it should be done, and how it should be approached. You must have answers, and this means having strong opinions about what is good, what is right, and what is true.

You need to have views and values that suggest that your dream client needs to do something different. You have to share your belief that one choice is better than another choice, that one course of action is better than another. You have to share your opinions on what these trends mean and what your client should be doing about them to prepare for the future, and this means change.

If it is true that baby boomers are retiring at the rate I have cited here throughout these examples, and if the talent pool is shrinking, then my view might be "Companies that are not building a recruiting plan to identify and hire replacements will fall behind in hiring the employees they need." My views and values here might sound like "Those companies that are not working to change their employee value proposition to appeal to younger generations will struggle, and this means flexible work hours, different perks, and a workplace that provides greater meaning and purpose." Another view I might share is that the hiring company needs to close the skills gap by building a training function that gives the younger people they are hiring the skills they need to succeed in their new role. I may express my values by saying that hiring people without giving them training is unfair. It will cause both the client and their new employee to fail. A salesperson who doesn't share my values might suggest that "it's the employee's duty to learn how to do their job," like they had to when they were coming up through the ranks.

These ideas are a response to the trends. They tell you what I think about the trends, as well as what you should be doing. They also express what happens if you do nothing, reinforcing the "why change now" message throughout all four of the different types of content and messaging you will use to begin to capture mindshare, create a case for change, and position yourself as a value creator, someone who can produce a better result.

You should not worry about your competitor gaining access to your ideas if you share them and your opinions with your dream clients. You cannot be known for having ideas that create value if no one knows that you have them. You can't displace your competitor by keeping your ideas secret. You also don't have to worry about other salespeople doing the work—or doing it consistently enough—to compete with you here. The approach I have described in the first three chapters of this book requires real work, and most of your competitors will not be willing to follow you down this path, preferring instead to sell at Level 1, hoping that their product, their company history, and their impressive logo will be enough to win them business, eliminating the need for them to occupy the role of peer and counsel.

SEQUENCING YOUR MESSAGE

This approach requires that you communicate consistently and that you professionally persist over time. To do so, you need a rock-solid plan. You also need to consider the sequence of your messages, what order you put things in to create a case for change, stacking one idea on top of another to build your case.

The ideas in this section provide you with a way of thinking about frequent communication and messaging. This is a recipe, which means it has certain ingredients. As with any recipe, you can modify it to your taste, but you can't change the ingredients completely without creating something different from the recipe. In this case, the core ingredients are what we have covered up to this point. You can change the frequency and sequence to match the needs of your business.

I like to start with a good round number of dream clients. For me, that number is sixty, simply because I can break that number into four groups and communicate over four weeks. The number sixty gives you a Group A, Group B, Group C, and Group D. You can choose a larger number, but unless you have a very, very small number of prospective clients, I wouldn't choose fewer than sixty.

Phone Call: The first week of the month, I will call, leave a voice mail, and send a follow-up email to my Group A. That call will sound very much like the dialogue I used earlier in this chapter, where I asked for a twenty-minute meeting to provide an executive briefing.

Voice Mail: Naturally, my dream clients are busy, so I will not reach many of the fifteen in Group A. I will leave a voice mail, explaining who I am, why I am calling, and what I want. I will close that voice mail by telling the client I am going to email them this message so that they have my contact information, and that I will call them back next week.

Email: The email I send will be short and to the point. I will apologize for missing my dream client, and I will let them know I'll call again next week to try to schedule an executive briefing. I will let them know my contact information is in the email, and that they can always reach out to me should they need anything.

Before we tackle Week Two, it's important to note that I did not ask my dream client to call me back. It isn't their job to call me back; I am pursuing their business, they're not pursuing me (this belief will save that fragile part of you that feels that you have somehow been rejected when your prospect doesn't call you back). I have also made it known that I will call back, which informs my dream client that I am serious about my pursuit of a meeting, that I am not one of those salespeople who call once a quarter and disappear. I am not going to be easy to wait out.

WEEK TWO—GROUP B

The second week of my campaign looks exactly like the first, this time calling, leaving a voice mail, and emailing Group B. The message doesn't change, only the group of prospective clients changes. But we also made commitments to Group A in Week One, and we now have to keep those commitments.

This pattern of call, voice mail, and email is used a second time with Group A. Now that they have missed your call, heard your voice, and received your email, you can modify your language, saying something like "Sorry I missed you again. I'll try to do better." You can start to be more personal, and more playful if you can. You don't want to be a bore and you don't want to be so serious that no one wants to take a meeting.

In Week Two, you will have called thirty target clients, either booked a meeting or having had a meeting request rejected, left voice mails, and sent emails to those you didn't reach. That is six calls and six emails a day. This leaves you plenty of time for additional prospecting and doing all the work necessary to capture the opportunities you are already working on.

WEEK THREE—GROUP C

This is the third week of the month, and this means Group C is being pursued using the exact same pattern you used with Groups A and B over the prior two weeks. Nothing changes but the group that gets added into the campaign. But you promised Group B you'd call again, so now you have to make those calls, too.

Having tried Group A two weeks in a row, you can mix it up a bit and send something of value with no ask—meaning you literally don't ask for anything, not even a callback. There are a lot of choices of content available to you here, as we have already outlined in this chapter.

- If you have a blog post that speaks to one of the trends that will impact your dream client's business, you share a link to that post, explaining why you believe it is important enough to command your dream client's attention (no more than two sentences).
- You can find a newspaper, magazine, or journal article that speaks to

the trend in some way that helps explain it. By printing the article for your dream client and highlighting the important parts, you are beginning the process of shaping their thinking and capturing mindshare. By deciding what deserves their attention, you are establishing yourself as an expert.

I would keep the early communications to "why change," even if you have to provide proof and facts and figures. To make this content speak to "why change," you have to write a couple lines explaining why this is important.

WEEK FOUR—GROUP D

You repeat the call, voice mail, email pattern with Group D. You owe Group C a follow-up call, and you will now send Group B the "why change" content you sent Group A last week. Having communicated with Group A three weeks in a row, you may give them a pause week, a week where you don't communicate. But not to worry, you are not going away, just leaving a little space. You want to be professionally persistent, not a pest, a nuisance, or someone who will end up receiving a restraining order from the local sheriff (no one should feel they need to look in their backseat to make sure you haven't been sitting in their car waiting for them to leave their workplace).

I want to give you some idea of what an overall approach might look like here, reminding you that the idea here is what matters. The pursuit of your dream client and capturing mindshare is a creative endeavor with a lot of room to play. But first, a word of caution.

You don't want to automate any of this. Period. Full stop. By attempting to automate these communications, you are undoing the intention here. The intention is for you to nurture the relationships you need, and relationships are not enhanced through automation. You are not trying to be efficient here; you are trying to be effective. These communications should have your fingerprints all over them. Either you care enough to do this work, or you don't. Your marketing department is never going to be your dream client's trusted counsel. You, on the other hand, are working to become just that.

The rest of the campaign might look like this:

Week Five

A: Call, voice mail, email
B: Pause week 1
C: Why change post or article
D: Call, voice mail, email

Week Six

A: LinkedIn connection
B: Call, voice mail, email
C: Pause week 1
D: Why change post or article

Week Seven

A: Pause week 2
B: LinkedIn connection
C: Call, voice mail, email
D: Pause week 1

Week Eight

A: Call, voice mail, email
B: Pause week 2
C: LinkedIn connection
D: Call, voice mail, email

Week Nine

A: Why change post or article 2

B: Call, voice mail, email

C: Pause week 2

D: LinkedIn connection

You've already provided one blog post or article that identifies a super trend and provided some content around "why change." You can introduce another trend here, or you can add additional context to the trend you have already identified. All of them will live under the theme you have identified in chapter 2.

Before we continue, I have a strong hunch (supported by my long experience) that this will be the most consistently you have ever pursued your dream clients in pursuit of a competitive displacement. It's doubtful that your competitor has ever had anyone work so persistently to gain a meeting with their client, and they have never had anyone work an approach based on value creation. This makes you a strong and dangerous competitor, even if it takes time, and even if you have to do this work while their existing contract runs out. So don't give up. Do the work.

Week Ten

A: Call, voice mail, email

B: Why change post or article 2

C: Call, voice mail, email

D: Pause week 2

Week Eleven

A: Pause week 3

B: Call, voice mail, email

C: Why change post or article 2

D: Call, voice mail, email

Week Twelve

A: Pause

B: Pause week 3

C: Call, voice mail, email

D: Why change post or article 2

WEEK THIRTEEN—ASSESS

At the end of this quarter of work, it makes sense to stop and measure your results. You also need to make adjustments. If you have communicated with your dream client eight times without getting so much as a response asking you to leave them alone, then you may want to change the stakeholder you are pursuing. If you have discovered that one of your dream clients isn't really a dream client at all, then you want to drop them from future campaigns.

This is the work of nurturing your dream clients and professionally pursuing them. This is how you become known as someone with the experience and ideas to make a difference. There is this old Chinese saying that if you want shade, the best time to plant a tree was a hundred years ago, and the second-best time is right now. The sooner you start this work, the sooner you will capture mindshare and create an opportunity. Even if your dream client isn't going to drop your competitor until there is an event, you want to be the first person they think of calling when that event occurs.

Competitive displacements don't happen overnight. You need to establish a long-term plan to nurture and develop relationships that position you for a competitive displacement. This work cannot be done sporadically, or without an intentional, well-designed pursuit plan—and the insights that lead to change.

DO THIS NOW

1. Make a list of resources you can use as part of your nurture campaign (Insights, Proof Providers, Facts and Figures, Views and Values).

2. Sketch out your thirteen-week campaign to nurture your dream clients.

   To download the worksheet that accompanies this chapter, go to www.eattheirlunch.training.

Chapter 4

PROSPECTING WITH THE INTENTION OF DISPLACEMENT

EVERYTHING IN THIS BOOK BEGINS AND ENDS WITH THE INTEN-
tion of displacing your competitor. The idea of differentiating on value creation is a large part of the strategy, and the plan to win mindshare and create the compelling case for change comprises the tactics that allow you to be known as a value creator and position yourself as your dream client's potential partner. The intention and the strategy of displacing your competitors extends to how you prospect.

Having established yourself as someone with ideas that can make a difference, you need to prospect in a way that invites your dream client contacts to agree to a meeting to explore change. This chapter will be every bit as practical and tactical as the prior chapters, so we can prepare to do the work of nurturing your dream clients and creating an opportunity.

DEVELOP A LIST OF DREAM CLIENTS

Winning your dream clients requires that you first determine the prospective clients and companies that will most benefit from your insights and your solutions. You are prospecting with the purpose of identifying and winning strategic clients.

Not all prospective clients are created equal. There are some prospective clients that are way more valuable to you and your company. These companies may spend more money than other companies. They may also be the premier prospective clients, the ones with the big, well-recognized logos (logos you are *not* going to use to impress other dream clients with, at least not during your first meeting).* They might also be the companies with the influencers who make it more likely that other companies in their space pay attention to you. But this is your side of the story, and while it is important that you select clients who make a difference to your business, you need to identify your dream clients by understanding their side of the relationship.

You and your competitors are not equal either. In some areas, you are far better than your competitors. In other areas, they might create value in a way that makes them the right choice for your dream client. Let me explain this with an example. Let's assume there is a big company in your territory that spends a lot of money in your category. It uses your product every day, and winning its business would drive up your revenue and make your entire annual quota. But your company focuses on compelling, differentiated value, and to deliver that value, you charge a higher price than your competitors (this story might start to sound familiar to you). This alleged dream client, however, is the low-price provider in their space, and their strategy is to squeeze their vendors and get the lowest price possible for everything they buy. Your irrational competitor has this client locked

---

* There are a lot of questions about sharing your current clients' logos as proof that you are credible or that the prospect is lagging the market. One risk in sharing big logos early is the risk of the client believing they are too small to be important to you. Another risk is that by doing so you shift out of Level 4 and back to Level 1, talking about your company and your clients instead of "why change." There are other, arguably better, ways to provide this evidence. One way you might consider is using the client name to talk about their view of the trend, why it caused them to change, and what they decided to do differently—with your help. Tying the discussion of the big-company logo to the message of compelling change can be helpful. But nothing is without risks, and you may have clients who will question working with you if you are deeply engaged with their primary rival.

down with a price there is no way you can come close to because it would be unprofitable business for you and your company. This eliminates this company from being a dream client. If they don't value what you sell enough to pay more, they are not a dream client. You know who these clients are either because you or someone in your company called on them at one time, or because these clients have a well-known reputation for squeezing their vendors.

If you are working your territory, you will know which of your competitors are serving which of your target companies. The more you prospect, the more information you gain. You can gain a lot of information by looking at the contact's LinkedIn profile. When they leave their network open, you can sometimes see who they are working with. When salespeople are short-sighted and overconfident enough to share their recommendations from clients, they make a good part of their client list available to you.

You might also know of companies with a similar need, an impressive logo, that spend a lot in your category but suffer from a leadership team that is immature, treating the companies they work with as "vendors" or "suppliers," not partners. They have difficult personalities, treat people poorly, and their immaturity as businesspeople makes them difficult to serve. They are what you might call "nightmare clients." If you haven't run across one of these, at some point you will. It won't matter how much they spend on what you sell; you will do everything you can to avoid them. Or you will suffer for taking their business, having to live with them and all of the baggage they bring with them. They're like caring for and feeding a pet dragon; from time to time, you are going to be badly burned. (And worse, you'll have to clean their cage.)

What are you looking for here? What makes a company a "dream client"? You are looking for companies that use what you sell strategically, meaning it is important to their business. This likely means they spend a lot in your category and are being affected by the trends you've identified—or soon will be. They will care about what you sell, and the ideas you have identified as being worth sharing will resonate with them. Most important, however, they will perceive what you do and how you do it as something that would make you a strategic partner, something more than a vendor or supplier. Because what you do creates more value, your dream clients will be willing to pay a higher price, allowing you to capture enough of the value you create that you can deliver the outcomes they need. What is key here is that they are trying to invest, not underinvest, in the results they need.

To create this list of dream clients, it makes sense to start with known prospective clients who spend a lot in your category. Their usage is an indicator, even if it isn't the only factor you need to consider. Some of the biggest and best clients you will ever find will be companies you may never have heard of that use what you sell strategically and spend as much as or more than some of the largest companies you call on.

CREATE PROSPECTIVE CLIENT TIERS

Not every prospect you call on will be a dream client. You still need to prospect, and that means you need to segment your time, segment your list, and deploy your limited time and energy appropriately to produce results.

The idea of targeting your dream clients for competitive displacements, eating your competitor's lunch by winning their business, provides focus. You are selecting the very best prospects for your campaigns—even though this list of prospective clients is cold, and even though these can be the most difficult clients to win. By doing so, you are deploying your time and effort toward an outcome—the displacement of a competitor and the acquisition of a meaningful client—that produces outsized results.

Putting time and effort into displacing your competitors in your dream client accounts will mean you are spending your time in a way that is 180 degrees different from your competitors'—and most salespeople's. Instead of avoiding the difficult to win clients that matter as most salespeople do, you will focus your time on the list of clients you know belong to your competitors, while they look for warm leads and potential prospects that won't require them to work very hard. This is the difference between proactively pursuing targets and reactively waiting for warm leads.

This doesn't mean you don't need to do additional prospecting. There are other prospective clients that, while being something less than a dream client, are still very good prospects. You need to pursue these clients, too. It makes sense to categorize your prospective clients to ensure that you are putting the appropriate effort into each category or segment.

Since we have already used the alphabet to describe the different groups of dream clients you will run quarterly campaigns against, we need to use a different nomenclature here. I'll use precious metals, but you can use whatever works for you.

- **Platinum**: These are your dream clients. Because these are your very best prospective clients, you'll focus your efforts here first. You might have 60 of these, or you may have 240. Your industry, your territory, and your goals will provide some guidance in determining how many of these you need. These are clients who will use what you sell strategically, will find it critical to their business, and will perceive the real value you offer.
- **Gold**: Not every prospect will be a dream client. Some, however, will come very close. Maybe they don't spend as much in your category, but they still use what you sell in large enough quantities to make them a very, very good prospective client. After prospecting to your dream clients, you want to spend time here next, knowing that some of these prospects will likely grow up to be dream clients.
- **Silver**: These prospects may not spend nearly as much in your category, and they will not use so much of what you sell as to make it a

strategic purchase. They are still solid prospects, and winning their business is an important part of reaching your goals. Spend your efforts here after you've done the work on higher-value prospective clients.

- **Bronze**: Small user, not strategic. This will make up the list of prospective clients who buy a little of what you sell, and because it isn't important enough to their business to command more of their time and investment, you are more likely to be perceived as a commodity. These prospective clients just don't have the kind of challenges at a great enough level for you to create the same level of value you create for your dream clients.

It would take many dozens of bronze (transactional) clients to make up the value of a single dream client, if that is even possible (and I doubt that it is; salespeople who hope to make their quota with small deals have to deal with many more clients with small problems and even smaller needs).

The rationale for segmenting your prospecting and your list is that you have limited time and energy. If you have sold for a while, you know that you can spend as much time winning a prospective client in the bronze category as one in the higher categories. So spend your time and energy on the things that produce the greatest return on investment.

The strategy and tactics I have played out in the first section of this book ensure that you spend your time first on your dream clients. If you have limited time, say ninety minutes, to prospect each day, you can very easily execute the ideas here against your list of dream clients. Your relentless, professional pursuit of your dream clients with a message around greater value creation and strategic outcomes will create opportunities to displace your competitors over time.

HOW TO RESEARCH YOUR PROSPECTIVE CLIENT

To make prospecting work, you have to separate the research from the actual prospecting and nurturing. There is a minimum viable amount of research that is required, and this is where you should start.

To develop an effective prospecting plan, you have to research the contacts within your dream client companies. It is important to know that research is necessary for prospecting, but it isn't prospecting. When you are researching, you aren't asking anyone for the commitment of time and a meeting to explore change, which precludes this from being actual prospecting. Because this is true, this activity needs to be separated from real prospecting. You want to do the research necessary to begin prospecting, and you want to do this work once, and in some format where you don't have to stop and research contacts to prospect effectively.

Some salespeople make too much of research, believing that they have to know everything about a contact and their company to make an effective call to schedule a meeting. It might be nice to know that your sister's husband went to the same college as a contact in your dream client's company, but it doesn't create any real value when you are prospecting. You aren't going to say, "I see you went to Wittenberg College. My sister's husband went there, too. We should meet."

Other salespeople make too little of research, not bothering to look at the company's website or the profile of the person they are trying to meet. This is negligent in a day and age when so much information is available, much of it self-disclosed. When people put their profile online, they are the ones typing in the content. This means that what they post is what they want other people to know about them. It makes no sense not to look at the company website and the profiles of the people you want to work with in the future. You might notice the person formerly worked for a company that is now your current client. That information may allow you to ask your current client to make an introduction or to share some insight about the new contact with you.

Here is the balance: minimal viable research. You want to do just enough research to be effective in prospecting and nurturing your dream clients. There are things you need to know to be able to prospect, and once you have that information, you can nurture and prospect within your dream client's company.

First, you need to know what the company does. When someone asks you, "Have you worked with a business like ours?" you don't want to answer, "And what does your business do?" Read the "about" page on the company's website and download a file you can drop in your CRM, so you don't have to go back and do this work again. Second, you need a list of contacts within this company. I believe it makes sense to start this process with titles of people you generally tend to sell to and work with. But there is one role that is often more important than the others, and I refer to this person as the CEO of the Problem, even though no one actually has that title.

I know you have been taught to go to the C-suite and let them push you down into their organization, but in most cases, the CEO doesn't care about what you sell. Moreover, they have people who work for them that they count on to make good decisions in their area, including the identification and acquisition of good strategic partners. The CEO of the Problem is the person with some authority who cares deeply about what you sell and the results that you produce. In your world, that could be the head of marketing, the vice president of sales, the IT director, or the head of maintenance. Whoever it is that cares enough about what you do and will own any initiative to change is the person you have to identify.

There are other people you will want to prospect to outside of the main title you call on. Because you are shaping their thinking, and because you are building mindshare, it makes sense to prospect to other roles within your dream client's company. It may feel subversive to bring more than one person into a potential conversation and explain to them how you can help them do better, and it is not without its risks. By calling every person you can find a number for, you can start to create a resistance within a group of people who may share with their peers the fact that they shut you down. Moreover, you may also draw so much attention to yourself that you put your competitor on notice. Ideally, you should run a campaign that tackles stakeholders one by one, and move on to new stakeholders only after you have established a strong line of communication with the first stakeholder or failed to get a meeting with them.

You are looking for people who use what you sell, the end users. You are also looking for people in departments outside of the primary area where you do work (your project might be led by IT, but if it offers access to data that marketing could use, you need to look for people in the marketing department). If someone will be positively affected by what you do, they are a potential contact. When you come into a dream client's company, you need to quickly move vertically (lower or higher within the department) and horizontally (to other departments) to find all the right stakeholders.

When you have identified the contacts for your pursuit plan, you need their contact information. You need a telephone number, an email address, and a physical address. This may be the most difficult part of all the research you need to do, and you may have to use a paid service to acquire some of the contact information.

This is minimally viable research. You need to do as much of this work as is necessary and no more. You should do it with the intention of completing the research once, capturing it all in a place where you know you can find it later, and updating it at most twice a year (or when events dictate you do more work).

DEVELOP A CONTACT PLAN

Your contact plan must be a multistakeholder approach to prospecting, covering both a horizontal and vertical view of your client contacts.

Earlier in this chapter I noted that you are looking for the CEO of the Problem, the person with the highest level of authority who cares deeply about what you sell and the improvement you can bring to their organization. I also hinted that you need to think about other stakeholders on the vertical, the people occupying different positions in one department or area of your client's business. You also need to think about the horizontal, the people in other departments who stand to gain something by moving from their existing supplier to you, a new strategic partner.

What I am going to share here goes against the conventional wisdom when it comes to prospecting, and I need to explain what has changed in sales that requires a new and different approach. For decades, you have been taught, told, and trained to call on the C-suite. The idea was to go to the person with authority to buy what you sell directly. By doing so, you'd have a chance to gain their support, the person with authority would push you down into the organization, and you would be able to use their support to create and win an opportunity. This used to be good advice. Today, gaining support from the C-suite is still necessary, but no longer sufficient.

Today, authority has been dispersed through the organization. Decisions are being made by consensus. The C-level executive you might have called in the past has no interest in what you sell unless and until the people who report to her have a strong interest in doing something different. C-level executives are less willing to mandate that their teams do something, because imposing a change—or a new supplier—on them creates resistance where they need buy-in. While you still need executive support, you are most likely to get it after being vetted by someone at a lower level of the organizational chart.

Now what you need is a way in. If someone will open the door and let you into the building, you can map out the company vertically and horizontally. If someone will open a window and sneak you into the building, you're in and you can figure things out from there. At one business I worked in, going through the front door meant going to human resources, where I was almost guaranteed to be shut down. Going through a window meant finding someone in another division who would engage and help bring in other stakeholders. A person with no real power who engages with you might not be the ideal place to start, but once you're in, you can make moves.

Your contact plan should start with a strong guess at who the CEO of the Problem might be (more on this later). You might be able to identify this person by their title or their role. Your first effort is to shape the thinking of this individual, knowing that they will be necessary to any decision to change. But if you struggle to make headway with this individual, you need to work on other options.

There are no right or wrong answers here, just choices. If you can't reach the CEO of the Problem, you can move down a level. There is solid logic in going lower in the organization before going higher. The people who are most likely to be struggling to produce the results they need and who would benefit from what you sell are levels down. The nurture campaign content you share will explain to them why they are struggling, and by bringing them to your cause, you increase the chances of a meeting. That said, your content and approach are now so strategic that if you get no traction with the CEO of the Problem, you can move up a level and start explaining the dissonance that the executive leadership is experiencing to them directly. If you have captured any information from people at lower levels in the organization, the conversation you have with the folks in the corner offices becomes much more real, and much more interesting. When you know where they are experiencing challenges, you can speak directly to these issues.

There are choices. No one right way guarantees success in all cases.

You want a list of contacts, of people in the area of your dream client's business where you primarily work, the people who care most about what you sell. You want contacts who are end users and those in leadership. This gives you more potential proponents on the inside. You also want contacts in the other departments that will be affected by any decisions to change, knowing that if they engage with you, your first order of business is to bring in people from the main department you serve.

BLOCKING TIME

You need a series of time blocks and a well-developed plan for prospecting enough to create enough of the right opportunities.

It is easy to assess a person's real goals by how they spend their time. The choices you make about what you do are a strong indicator of what you really want. The consistency of the action you take is an even stronger indicator. If you really want to take your dream clients away from your competitors, the evidence will be visible to all who watch what you are doing.

The first third of this book is about creating greater value to create a competitive mismatch, developing the insights that allow you to capture mindshare, turning those ideas and insights into an actual plan to nurture your dream clients and pursue a relationship, and prospecting with the intention of displacing your competitor—that is, eating their lunch. For these strategies and tactics to work, you have to block time to consistently do the work.

The only real secret to productivity is to spend your time doing what is most important until completion. Productivity isn't measured by the hours you work or how many tasks you cross off your to-do list. It's measured by the results you produce on the most important outcomes you need to achieve. The way that you ensure that you produce those outcomes is by blocking time.

In chapter 3, I outlined the idea of selecting sixty dream clients to pursue. Splitting that number into four groups (one for each week of the month) provides you with fifteen prospective clients to call each week (even though the plan I outlined in chapter 3 recommends more activity). If you followed up each call with an email that provides some insight, you would literally be making three calls each day, followed by three emails. That might take you all of twenty minutes.

Blocking ninety minutes a day for nurturing and pursuing your competitors' best clients to make them your own is transformational. If you want to take your dream clients away from your competitors, that outcome requires an investment of time and energy. If you want to steal your dream client away, you must be willing to do more work to make that true than your competitor will do to retain them. If you want to win big takeaways, you have to put forth the effort. Deploy enough time and energy toward any outcome, and all obstacles eventually yield.

THE COMMITMENT FOR TIME AND EXPLORATION

Creating the opportunity to displace your competitor begins only when you gain the commitment of time (see *The Lost Art of Closing*). The time, energy, and resources you deploy toward the goal of capturing your dream client's attention, helping them understand the need to change, and proving that you are someone with the ideas and ability to help them navigate their way to a better future is what allows you to gain this commitment.

The process of a competitive displacement begins when you have a meeting to explore change. This is the first crack, and when done well, it is the starting point of a displacement.

DO THIS NOW

1. Make a list of your platinum dream clients. If you are unsure how many to include, start with the number sixty.

2. Research these clients, identifying three contacts within each company whom you will professionally pursue to begin the process of a displacement.

3. Drop three ninety-minute blocks on your calendar for prospecting inside your competitor's clients.

   To download the worksheet that accompanies this chapter, go to www.eattheirlunch.training.

PART 2

BUILDING CONSENSUS: WIRE THE BUILDING

To win your dream client's business, you first have to win the hearts and minds of the contacts within that business. This is not limited to the single contact who supports your effort and is willing to help you find your way around their company, the receptive one providing you with information and introductions. To displace your competitor, you need to go wide and deep.

In *The Lost Art of Closing*, I wrote that the buyer doesn't have a map, they *are* the map. In the second part of this book, we will look at the maps—the different stakeholders' individual and collective maps of the organization—in order to develop a plan to wire the building.

Chapter 5

HELPING YOUR DREAM CLIENTS DISCOVER SOMETHING ABOUT THEMSELVES*

IN THE PAST, THE IDEA OF "DISCOVERY" MEANT ASKING YOUR client about the areas where they were presently dissatisfied, the areas where they were aware they were struggling to produce results. The idea here was that by talking about what are called pain points, the things that were causing your prospective client problems, you could create an opportunity, a chance to win their business. There is nothing inherently wrong with this idea, and it was how we successfully sold for decades.

But as the business economy is still being reshaped by forces like globalization (which brings more and greater competition), disintermediation (in which technology disrupts and displaces the middleman in transactions), and commoditization (low barriers of entry, a glut of competitors, and decreasing differentiation), the approach of asking your prospective client questions about their dissatisfaction has lost a good bit of its effectiveness—especially if they already have someone selling them what you sell. Now your clients are less likely to want to answer questions

---

* This chapter is one of the more powerful concepts in the book, and it can be difficult to understand. Please go to eattheirlunchbook.training/chapter 5 for a video tutorial to learn to apply this to your opportunities.

designed to elicit their pain. They've learned to live with their problems, as difficult as they are. The status quo often seems safer than a decision to do something different in a world of constant, accelerating, disruptive change, even if that's exactly the wrong—and most dangerous—response.

The world today is very different from the world in which your parents grew up. In almost every way it is better, but it is also more difficult. This is nowhere truer than in business, with whole industries being transformed, seemingly overnight. Netflix has completely obliterated Blockbuster by streaming video directly to consumers on their devices, and it wouldn't be too much to say that it is now doing the same to traditional television broadcasters. Uber is displacing taxis. Facebook has changed what it means to be a publisher and how most people spend their free time. General Electric, which was the darling of US business my entire adult life, is now in the throes of figuring out its place in the economy, something I would never have imagined as a possibility. I could go on—the examples are endless.

What all of this points to is that the effectiveness of traditional discovery has declined over time. It is far less likely that the customer you are trying to take from your competitor knows what they need to improve, understands their choices around the changes they should make, or has the experience to make those changes. Even if a few contacts are aware of their challenges and have opinions of what they need to do, they view those challenges through their limited experience. While you sell and execute your solution across many companies, their experience is usually limited to a single company. Your discovery work needs to address the entire organization and not just a few dissatisfied stakeholders. Business is more difficult, and the challenges greater and more systemic. Discovery needs a framework that takes a more holistic view of the client and their place in a changing business ecosystem.

If you want to make real change, one that includes swapping out your competitor, you must have a greater understanding of what needs to change and a clearer view of the people who need to make those changes.

This is what allows you to see something your competitor doesn't see—and helps your client discover something about themselves. Let's look at what discovery looks like in the age of value creation.

A CLEARER LENS THROUGH WHICH TO SEE YOUR CLIENT

Consultative selling requires a greater level of discovery. A surface-level discovery of pain points is not enough to compel change, nor is it enough to help your client make the necessary changes to produce better results. This is why we developed the case for change in chapter 2. This chapter will introduce a new form of discovery, one unlike any you have ever been taught before. This approach is based on integral theory, a framework developed by Ken Wilber.

Integral theory starts with the premise that everything in our world is made up of holons, or wholes that are made up of parts, which in turn are wholes in themselves. Wilber's great insight is that all holons have interiors and exteriors, and they are both individual and part of a collective. The result is that everything has an individual interior and exterior, as well as a collective interior and exterior. This framework is incredibly useful when trying to develop a holistic view of a large and complex organization, and the individuals within it. You may have heard about the shoe retailer Zappos's move to an organizational structure without managers. That idea, called holarchy, is derived from this central idea.

The holons have an interior and exterior component, as well as being an individual and part of a collective, making up four quadrants. Now, let's make this both simple to understand and useful by looking at you.

Individual Interior: Your individual interior is made up of your thoughts, your ideas, your values, your feelings, your psychology. This is your subjective view, and it includes things like your values, your purpose, your motivations, and what things mean to you.

HOLONS

INDIVIDUAL

INTENTIONAL	**BEHAVIORAL**
· VALUES	· KEY PERFORMANCE INDICATORS (KPIs)
· STATUS	· METRICS
· LEVELS	· ACTIVITIES
· TYPES	· BEHAVIORS
· MOTIVATION	
· PREFERENCES	

INTERIOR   **EXTERIOR**

CULTURE	**SYSTEMS**
· SHARED VALUES	· ORG. STRUCTURE
· PURPOSE	· SYSTEMS
· WORLDVIEW	· PROGRAMS
· PRIORITIES	· STRATEGY
· INTENTIONS	· MARKETING

COLLECTIVE

Individual Exterior: You also have an individual exterior, including a body and a brain. You are doing things that we can see, take account of, and measure. These are objective facts, with metrics and statistics that are bound to the laws of physics. This is what behavioral science measures.

Collective Interior: You also have a collective interior, which we might call culture. You belong to groups, like a country, a business, or a church, where you have shared values. Many of the values you have individually were installed through your collective interiors. We are all part of tribes.

Collective Exterior: Last, you have a collective exterior. You live in a shared social system, a shared environment, and a shared economy.

I made this example about you because it's the easiest place to start. I also greatly simplified the idea, to make it practical and tactical. Now let's use this lens to see your dream client differently, and then we'll discuss how to use it to get a more complete view of change.

WHAT CAN YOU SEE?

There is a reason that it is difficult for your dream clients to change. The four quadrants provide us with a much clearer view as to what needs to change and how to help people and companies make those changes. Here is a hypothetical example.

Individual Interior: A leader just took over a manufacturing facility. His overriding value is the safety of the employees who work in his facility. When faced with a decision, he will err on the side of safety, even if it slows production, and even if that means the rest of the organization needs to make changes to accommodate his directive. In his last role, working in an industrial manufacturing facility, these beliefs resulted in improvements in safety and increased the quality of life for the workers, increased profits, and resulted in his promotion.

To elicit this information, we have to access this contact's interior by asking him questions. This is how humans work to understand one another.

Individual Exterior: The leader begins to make and implement new safety rules, frustrated with his progress. When some rule isn't implemented, he adds additional rules to try to achieve the outcome he needs, only to have every attempt greeted with contempt and resistance, most of it unspoken. His team tries to wait him out, as frustrated with him as he is with them.

To discover this information, we have to look for what this contact is doing. How do his beliefs manifest in his world? Beliefs lead to actions and actions lead to outcomes, good or bad. What you discover here is what you can objectively see and measure. Outcomes often lead to beliefs, too.

Collective Interior: The new leader's values are in conflict with the rest of the organization, in which speed to market has heretofore been the core value. The organization resists the new leader's focus on safety, pointing to the fact that they have the best safety record in the company already. The leader's team resists his efforts and drags their feet, working hard to wait him out.

Gaining this information is a matter of asking questions and making observations across a number of contacts, collecting their stories, and uncovering the group's values and beliefs.

Collective Exterior: The company the leader works for is in retail fashion. The industry winners have focused on speed to market as a way to gain competitive advantage. Slowing down the process of creating new offerings means losing to other faster, more agile competitors. Furthermore, the leadership team is compensated on their results, so faster means greater personal earnings.

The exterior is made up of the systems and processes that the company uses to generate results.

You can inform what you know here by researching your client and their industry and collecting data points throughout your conversation with contacts inside the company. You can also leverage what you know from your experience helping other companies.

If you were calling on the leader in this hypothetical example, you would be thrilled to learn that he is dissatisfied with the status quo, is compelled to change, and is looking to buy things and work with people who can help him with his safety initiatives. Eliciting his individual interior (his pain points) would be enough to convince you that you have an opportunity and that you can make a difference with your safety-related solution. Eliciting his individual exterior, what he is doing, would only convince you further that he will be your client. He continues to do things without getting the result he needs, and he wants help.

You may not, however, have looked at the collective interior or exterior, and by not doing so, you will have overlooked the real challenge in making change. The leader is at odds with the existing culture over values.

He wants to be a change agent, and he wants to make a difference, but the rest of the organization has a different, deeply ingrained belief system. He is also at odds with where the business is positioned in the competitive landscape (the collective exterior). Providing the right solution here would mean providing something that improves the already excellent safety record while increasing speed, or at least not slowing things down. Knowing that this is what is necessary requires that you look at the problem from Level 4, a strategic view that includes "what must change and why?" A salesperson with a narrow view, one constrained to meetings with the leader, will struggle to understand how to make change—and will find it incredibly difficult to build consensus around that change.

Why is this approach so useful to competitive displacement? If you can see what others cannot, you will find opportunities they miss. If what is invisible to your competitor is visible to you, you will see solutions where they see only unresolvable challenges. The very heart of discovery work is the exploration of change and the collaboration and consensus around a solution. This more complete view of discovery provides a better, deeper understanding. It also allows you to help the client discover something about themselves.

DISCOVERY IN ALL FOUR QUADRANTS

Let's look at all four quadrants and how you might elicit and use what you learn to create an opportunity to displace your competitor and win your dream client's business.

One of the things we salespeople are very good at is finding a single individual and discovering what they want and need and prefer. One of our primary skill sets as professionals is being able to engage in a conversation that allows us to see things that can't easily be seen, especially individual interiors. When we have early meetings with our prospective clients, most of what we are eliciting is subjective. We want to know what the person sitting across from us believes, what they want, and why they want it. We want to know their personal and business motivations. We want to understand how to align with these subjective beliefs and preferences, and what we can do to serve the client, hence our directive to win mindshare and create a preference to work with us.

If you've been selling for any length of time, you have been doing this work the whole time, even if you didn't know it. In this section, you will learn to see things you haven't seen before and understand how to better use what you learn. The following list includes the things that you elicit to give you a map of the individual contact to help you better understand who they are.

INDIVIDUAL INTERIORS

Values and Ethics

How do you engage with the person you are attempting to have a discovery conversation with? Understanding their value system is a useful place to start. There are a lot of frameworks for examining an individual's values and beliefs. I find Wilber's to be the most complete, since it is a composite of dozens of others.* Here we are going to look at the four types of individual interiors that are relevant and useful for our purposes. All of us are capable of occupying all of the types below, at different times and under different situations, but you will find that individuals have a stronger tendency toward one or the other.

- Red: This level of values is focused on self-empowerment, opportunity seeking, self-promotion, boundaries, and the development of conceptual

---

* Other frameworks on looking at an individual's interiors include those of Abraham Maslow, Jane Loevinger, Robert Kegan, and Lawrence Kohlberg, as well as Clare Graves's spiral dynamics.

thinking. But this level isn't all positive, as it also brings a self-interest and self-orientation and the desire to use power to further one's self-interest.

A contact who is mostly red will be determined and forceful, but may also be difficult to work with, especially when they don't get what they want. Many of us enter this state when we are under stress. When approaching a person who is red, you want to approach them with ideas as if they were already aware of them, you want to frame your ideas as benefiting them and their wants and needs, and you'll want to be careful when engaging in conflict. Challenging their views can cause them to disengage or actively work against you.

• Amber: Amber individuals are able to take the role of the other, the second-person perspective that empathy is built upon. At this stage, you start to identify with groups, sacrifice what you want for the good of others, and practice belonging, conviction, order, and behavior that is appropriate for the group.

As it pertains to a competitive displacement and creating a preference, people with this value system can be difficult, believing that there is only one right way. When you are aligned with what they want, you are easily preferred. Later, you may find that their rigidity and inability to consider new ideas create challenges. Your competitor may be struggling with them for this very reason. You'll know a person at this level by the fact that they see very little gray. Things are wrong or right, black or white. You may find it helpful to work above this person to establish a new paradigm so that this person believes some new idea is now true for them. Alternatively, these people can be very helpful if they believe your competitor is "wrong."

• Orange: The value level of the achiever, the rugged individual. You act in your own self-interest, you work to advance yourself and grow, you look for the way to maximize your results, and you are generally optimistic. You develop the ability to look at yourself objectively and take a third person's perspective. This is the rational, scientific type. This is the strategist who looks for competitive advantages. You will run into this value system quite a bit in sales and in business. Many entrepreneurs share this individual interior.

People at this level tend to be growth oriented and are often open to new ideas that will help them improve their results. They can also come across as hard-charging and demanding in pursuit of those goals. You are used to dealing with people at this level. They are looking for logical ideas and solutions. They are driven by results, and they like to see objective proof that what you are proposing will work. They also tend to have a need for importance and the accompanying signals.

• Green: This is the sensitive, egalitarian type. Individuals with this interior are all about caring and community. This type places a greater focus on consensus and harmony and human development. You see cultures with leaders at this level in places like Whole Foods and Zappos, and reflected in ideas like those of Simon Sinek.

As more people share this value system, the more you will see consensus as key to displacing a competitor. People with this value system will want to bring more people into the conversation. They will also tend to continue with the status quo when consensus isn't easily reached. Your approach to people at this level needs to prioritize consensus, inclusion, values, and contribution. They care about the impact of the decisions they make on the communities they serve and the environment. You help by assisting them in making a contribution.

A person's level is a large part of the lens through which they view their world. If you've been in sales for a significant period of time, you've no doubt run across individuals at different levels.

Let's take a look at how this works in practice:

The hard-charging, growth-oriented contact who wants to make change is likely orange. When he doesn't get what he wants, he resorts to red strategies, using force and his formal authority to make people do what he wants instead of leveraging his moral authority and influence to produce results. You help this person when you propose strategies that get him what he wants without resorting to the poor strategies on which he sometimes relies.

Your hard-charging orange is often at odds with his green counterpart, the one who always wants to ensure that everyone has a place at the table, that everyone is heard, and that they reach consensus before moving forward. This contact is concerned with excluding people and can see each person's side of an issue. You help this person by enabling the process of bringing in other stakeholders—and by helping them understand that consensus doesn't require unanimity.

The amber stakeholder, the manager who will be charged with executing your solution, doesn't want to change because there are already rules and regulations in place. She is concerned with stability and the one right way to produce the outcome. Her view is "We've done things this way for a long time, it can't possibly be wrong." You help this person with change when you establish systems and processes that need to be followed and provide the structure she needs.

The map here is not the terrain. It is, however, useful in understanding who people are, what they need, and how you can help them get what they want. Your competitor, meanwhile, has no idea why their clients believe and behave as they do, and with this little bit of information, you can now see more than they can.

Lines of Development

One of the most important discoveries in the last century was that human beings possess multiple intelligences (an idea popularized by Howard Gardner in a book titled *Frames of Mind*). There are now dozens of intelligences, but the ones we are most concerned with here include cognitive intelligence, emotional intelligence, and moral intelligence.

- **Cognitive Intelligence:** People with high cognitive lines (IQ) are smart. You often find these people in leadership roles because they are intelligent. These people tend to have a greater depth of understanding of how things work, and they tend to have a desire to learn, to seek additional information and additional perspectives.

You will have contacts who may not be as high on the cognitive line as others, but who have deeper experience and situational knowledge that levels the playing field. Some are hugely ambitious, with a drive and an appetite that allows them to build big businesses—and surround themselves with people who know things they don't.

- **Emotional Intelligence:** Emotional intelligence (EQ) is made up of two fundamental parts. The first part is interpersonal intelligence, or the idea that you understand other people's emotions, motivations, intentions, and desires. If you are in sales, this is a capacity you need in large measure, and you'll need to be able to identify it in others. The second part is intrapersonal intelligence, which is the ability to understand your own emotions, feelings, motivations, and fears.

The idea of emotional intelligence has been criticized as not being an intelligence at all, with some seeing it as a skill. Others have suggested that the measurement doesn't correlate to better performance in managerial roles. But for our purposes, we don't need to worry about whether or not it is an intelligence. We are looking at this to understand the person sitting across from us during a sales meeting, so that we can better calibrate how we serve them in the process of changing.

People with higher emotional intelligence on the whole tend to be able to take another person's perspective. They can put themselves in another's place, recognizing how they might feel about something, what they might need, and how they are likely to respond. A lower EQ suggests that the person will have a more difficult time taking another person's perspective.

A word of caution here: These categories are being used to create a map to help you understand your clients and prospective clients. The categories are not designed for you to judge people. Different people have different strengths. The fact that someone is high or low on one of these two lines doesn't suggest that they are better or worse than someone else. Which brings us to another line that makes this point clear.

- **Moral Intelligence**: Lest you be tempted to think IQ and EQ together make someone superior, you might be surprised to learn that Adolf Hitler had both a high IQ and a high EQ. He was smart, and he was able to persuade large groups of people by understanding a group of people's perspectives. He is also one of a small handful of people who caused so much death and destruction that his very name defines a category. Moral intelligence matters as much as or more than the others—especially when you are going to be working with someone for a long time!

Moral intelligence is the ability to understand right and wrong. When people get in trouble, it's because they make bad legal or ethical decisions. People who are low on the moral line can be dangerous. I've had a prospective client in one business tell me that in order to win their account I would have to pay them directly and suggested I raise my rates to cover their kickback. This was a moral mismatch, and it precluded us from doing business together. If a person is willing to steal from their own company, they're not going to be a good long-term partner. Of the three lines we've looked at here, this one tends to present the types of problems that are easiest to avoid. You just walk away from people who would put you at risk by doing things that are illegal or unethical.

A person with a very high cognitive line and a very low emotional intelligence will be very smart about a lot of things but have a very difficult time working with other people. A person with the opposite attributes may have an easy time working with other people but may need help understanding complex concepts and ideas. You may need to spend more time with them or change your approach to sharing ideas to better serve them.

INDIVIDUAL EXTERIORS: BEHAVIORAL OBSERVATIONS—WHAT ARE THEY DOING NOW?

This level of discovery deepens our understanding by looking at what the individual is actually doing. These are the physical manifestations of their interiors. The behaviors are what we can see and measure.

They are the actions a contact is taking, the results they are producing (or not producing, as the case may be), and the visible evidence available to you. Having done discovery as we have traditionally done it for decades now, you're almost certain to be pretty good at discovering the individual exterior, even if you didn't have these labels.

If you have been in sales for any time, you know what you are looking for here. The client tells you that they need to improve some metric, be it revenue, costs, profit, throughput, market share, speed to market, better responsiveness from their partner, greater communication, or any number of outcomes that might be improved.

If you want to create a case for change and take your competitor's client from them, your ability to understand the interior and exterior of individuals will give you deeper insights into how to better compel that change. You want to understand their subjective beliefs, values, wants, and needs. You also want to know what they are doing, and the result it is generating.

A friend of mine has a business in which he was struggling with his sales force. He believed that they were no good at presenting and negotiating. That was his subjective belief. The objective truth was that they were responding to requests for proposals instead of generating their own opportunities. His sales team believed that they shouldn't have to prospect, that they should wait for potential deals to come to them. His team's beliefs and behaviors were the root of this problem, and it had nothing whatsoever to do with his beliefs (individual interior). Had he trained his team on presenting and negotiating, it would not have improved their performance. The evidence proved this to be true.

COLLECTIVE INTERIOR: SHARED BELIEFS AND CULTURES

One of the reasons so many change efforts fail is because the salesperson and their company don't do the work necessary to understand their prospective client's collective reality, their culture, their view of their world. This is now necessary to help create the case for change and to build consensus.

- **Collective Worldview**: If there is an area where we struggle in sales, it is understanding the collective values of the company. It can be difficult to pick up what the real shared values are, especially if you meet with only a few stakeholders. And it is rare that the real collective values are found in the mission or vision statement on their lobby wall. Going back to Ken Wilber's work, a red culture is one where the organization believes that their suppliers are their enemy, as are their competitors and clients (think of the movies *Glengarry Glen Ross* or *Wall Street*). A culture that is green will look very different, with the outcomes to employees, clients, and external stakeholders being considered (think *Star Trek* and the Prime Directive, also Zappos and Whole Foods).

- **Collective Values:** The collective interior also includes a collective worldview. This worldview is made up of the collective experience of the organization and the dominant interpretation of events and their meaning. It's a collective map. That map might suggest that "Our clients need us, and we are here to serve them" or "Our clients are all difficult with unrealistic expectations." What people believe has an impact on the results they produce, but it has an even greater impact on their ability to change.
- **Stories and Identity:** The collective interior is also made up of the shared stories of the organization and the organization's identity. One of the most popular stories about Apple is a Steve Jobs statement that helped solidify their identity: "We're here to put a dent in the Universe. Otherwise, why else even be here?" These stories help shape the collective interior, the values and worldview.

When you are helping a company and the people who work there to change, you are working with individuals and the collective—even if you haven't had a framework before for naming the collective interior. You have, no doubt, run into change initiatives and deals that you have sold that failed specifically because the collective culture rejected the change. The levels that are included in the individual interior also produce a center of gravity in the collective.

COLLECTIVE EXTERIOR: ELICITING POSITION AND STRATEGY, OPPORTUNITIES AND THREATS

The collective exterior is made up of things like the company's organizational structure, its process, and initiatives like Six Sigma and other systems. The most interesting part of the collective exterior for our purposes is where it rubs against the market, the economy, and the competition. The company's strategy falls into this category. It's how it intends to compete and win.

When we looked at the individual interior, we did so to better understand an individual. The same is true when we looked at individual exteriors. The collective interior is cultural, and that is one of the keys to understanding what might change and what you and your dream client need to do to make change—and displace your competitor. Now we are looking at what the prospective client is doing and the results they are producing to determine why they struggle to produce results and what we can do about it.

Even if this sounds complicated, it isn't. We've already done some of the work throughout the first third of this book. We can bounce off that work to make this actionable now. Remember when we talked about the baby boomers retiring? The company's collective exterior might be the system they use to attract and retain the talent they need. That talent acquisition system might be the very thing that is causing our hypothetical company challenges in producing the results they want because the system isn't working to attract the candidates they need.

Here's another example. Let's say a sales organization is struggling to produce results. Maybe their sales process was developed in the 1980s, when it might have made sense to be transactional. That process, the collective exterior, is what is driving the behaviors in the individual exterior—and bumping up against a market that rejects that approach in favor of greater value creation. Let's stay with this example and go a little further. Maybe the leader of the sales organization believes that transacting is the right thing to do, and maybe it is what allowed him to succeed when he was in sales. The collective culture might be built on the belief that "clients need to be pushed hard" and that they "can't be allowed to win in a negotiation." This is one single challenge, and you can see how it touches all four of the quadrants.

Every part of the business is a system, from marketing, to human resources, to finance and accounting, to operations. This deeper, more holistic view of the client and the company allows you to do real discovery, and it massively improves your ability to create real change. Furthermore, it is the deeper view of what your dream client needs to do to produce better results that provides you with the insights on what needs to change and how that change needs to be implemented inside your dream client. This knowledge is critical to a competitive displacement. The super trends in chapter 2 can help you understand the collective exterior.

MAKING THE FOUR QUADRANTS TACTICAL AND PRACTICAL

Let's look at a marginally hypothetical example here to bring all this to life, one in which a new leader needs to make change in his company.

Who Is This Person?

Let's look at a real stakeholder and see how we might understand him and use what we know to help him discover something about himself and his company. Let's say this leader has orange values. The lens he looks through will be a rational view, and he will probably look for evidence that what you say is true. He'll likely believe that his destiny is in his own hands, and that he can achieve his goals. A person with these values seeks competitive advantages and may be drawn to that kind of thinking. Most noticeable, however, is his high need for significance. All his advanced degrees hang behind him on the wall, and on his desk is a picture of his wife and his expensive red convertible.

Your approach may be to protect his ego, knowing that sharing ideas he may not have considered may be seen as an attack that requires him to defend his ego. Instead of sharing information as if it is news to him, you may start by saying, "A lot of what I am going to share with you will be our view of some of the things you are likely tracking, too. I'd like to ask you to share your thoughts on our thinking here. I'd love to get your perspective."

What Is He Doing?

We may also know something about this stakeholder's individual exterior. He was hired by the CEO, who asked him to turn around a department that was failing. He fired two managers in the first thirty days and spent the next sixty days really learning the business. You know this because he told you, as did all the people you have communicated with inside the company. You've also heard that he has put together a plan for every part of the department and has shared it only with the leadership team, leaving most people concerned that real change is coming—and that it will be unpleasant.

Interiors give insight into exteriors, and vice versa. Knowing who you are dealing with helps you understand why they are doing what they are doing. Let's continue through the other two quadrants to make sure you know how to use this framework.

Who Are the Collective?

This leader works within a culture that was once positive and optimistic. This team worked with a value system that was more green than orange. Everyone treated one another with respect, and they strove to make decisions together that served the organization. But as their business faced difficult challenges, some of the leaders left, and the culture started to deteriorate. It's now descended into a red culture, with everyone jockeying for position, trying to save themselves—even at the expense of others. Power is now the currency.

What can you do with this information? How can you use it? If you are consultative, you can address the leader in this hypothetical and say, "I am concerned that people who work here are going to be afraid of the changes that you need to make. How can we engage them so they know what we're doing and how it will serve them?" Or you might say, "In other turnarounds, we've sometimes seen it make sense to build a team that will carry the message and lead their peers, helping them understand why these changes are necessary and how we're going to ensure that they succeed. Could something like that help here?"

What Are They Doing?

The root cause of this department's problem is that the technology they have used for decades no longer allows them to be competitive. It's too slow, and the quality of work it produces is inferior to the market that long ago moved on. They're competing with analog equipment in the digital age. Additionally, the industry has been commoditized, and they've lost their ability to differentiate in any positive way (they're plenty different, just all in a bad way).

You sell the equipment that would modernize and breathe new life into this company. The investment in equipment will be significant, and selling it to them would help them. But their existing staff would have to be retrained, and their sales and marketing would have to change to make use of their new capabilities to acquire customers and orders.

There are Level 1 salespeople who would look at this scenario and believe that they should simply sell the equipment to this leader. These salespeople would not focus on the strategic outcome of making real change, believing their duty is only to sell him equipment—even if it fails to produce the necessary result. Level 4 salespeople, in contrast, believe that they should sell the equipment, the training, and also consult with the company's marketing team to help them learn how to position the company to sell effectively after buying the equipment. These salespeople would understand that they are making change inside a complex organization, and would look at this problem holistically. The first salesperson wouldn't see the same picture as the second salesperson. The Level 1 salesperson, having a very narrow understanding of the problem, would start with slides about their company and their product. The Level 4 salesperson would focus on the client and title their presentation "Reclaiming XYZ's Category Dominance," something I suspect the stakeholder might recognize as his vision.

That conversation sounds like this: "The equipment itself won't get you everything that you want. We're going to retrain and retool your team, and we'll need to work with marketing to help them change what they're doing so you can crank up the revenue. This is a plan for a fast recovery and for repositioning XYZ on top."

Now that you understand what you are seeing, you can begin to create an opportunity for a competitive displacement.

DO THIS NOW

1. Make a list of three contacts you know well inside your existing client accounts.

2. Write down what you know about their values and preferences. Then write down what they do because they have those values and beliefs.

3. Write down what the culture of their company looks like and what signs indicate that that culture exists. Then write down what the company is doing that might be creating a strategic challenge in the future.

To download the worksheet that accompanies this chapter, go to www.eattheirlunch.training.

Chapter 6

CREATING OPPORTUNITIES

SOMETIMES OPPORTUNITIES ARE CREATED WHEN YOUR DREAM client experiences some event that makes "good enough" no longer good enough. The last chapter gave you a new way to take a deeper, more holistic view of your client's business and their challenges and opportunities. That deeper discovery allows you to see something that other salespeople don't—and something that is mostly invisible to your clients. That knowledge allows you to ask questions in a way that separates you from other salespeople and positions you to make a competitive displacement. When you have a deeper understanding, you establish yourself as the person who can see the change and the person who knows what must be done and how to do it.

DEVELOPING A VISION OF A BETTER FUTURE

No one changes until they believe they have a good reason to, and even then, some refuse to change until they are compelled by outside events. You create opportunities when you help your clients develop a vision of the better future available to them, show them what is possible, and help them understand how to get there. That makes you the catalyst for change.

What your dream client needs you to answer for them is "What do I get on the other side of this change? What will the future look like?"

The way you want to set up this strategy is to define the current state, define the future state, and then define the solution that will be necessary to move your client from the current state to the better future state they need. Let's go back to the example we used at the end of the last chapter, where the stakeholder is struggling to turn around the failing department. The conversation might sound like this:

Current State: "The current state is that you are struggling to win new sales because your equipment is antiquated and doesn't allow you to generate the outcomes your clients need now. The market share erosion is being caused by new technologies that produce better results at a lower price. The team is afraid there will be job losses, and they're concerned about whether their department is going to survive."

Future State: "You will have the new technologies to compete against your rivals with a product that exceeds the quality of work they create at the same or lower price. Your team has been trained to use the new equipment, and they've been skilled up to compete with anyone, anywhere, anytime. Your marketing and sales enablement departments have the ability to help your sales force win back lost clients as well as create new opportunities."

It is helpful if you can frame the solution in a way that gives you a clear and compelling advantage, but that isn't always possible. The challenge in being a value creator is that there is no way to be a trusted adviser without the advice. Even though there are risks, because you have taught your client how to think about their challenges and how to move to the future state, there is greater likelihood that they'll want you to do the work of helping to execute the solution. There is always the possibility, however, that you teach your dream client how to teach your competitor to produce a better outcome. That is the risk you must accept to play the game now.

Solution: "To achieve these outcomes, we are going to install the XO348, the technology with the fastest production, the highest-quality output, and the lowest cost per unit. We will then train your team to use this new technology, while consulting with your marketing and sales teams to help them position you to create new opportunities within your past client base and the future clients this transformation will open up to you."

This sounds like your final presentation, and it very well might be. But when you are creating an opportunity, this is the very conversation you need to have. You need to close by asking the question "Does it make sense to do this now, and can we get the support we need to make this kind of change?"

How do you get to this stage in the sales conversation? How do you get to a well-defined vision of the future?

You start by sharing what you believe that might look like based on what you know about your client and what you know from your experience helping other companies produce better results. You also ask questions to allow your dream client contacts to help you define what is possible.

You say, "Based on the conversation we've had up to this point, I believe that making the changes we've discussed around improving your throughput will result in a production increase of just over fifteen percent and will eliminate the overtime hours you are paying for now due to the rework you have to do. What do you think?"

There is a good reason to ask your dream client what they think about the potential results. I have shared my thoughts on results and the client's return on investment only to have them tell me I underestimated the value of the solution, that their internal calculations prove the solution is much more valuable. We used their larger ROI instead of our more conservative numbers to make the case for change. You will also have clients who go the other way, suggesting they aren't sure they can get to the future you're describing, in which case you have more work to do in helping them see that future. You start by saying, "What do you see?"

This idea of collaboration is important. How you get to the future state matters as much as what that future state looks like. You need to invite your dream client into a collaborative conversation by saying something that sounds like "I think one way we might get the results we are talking about here is to change out one piece of equipment and change your start-up process. Tell me what you think about that and how we might make this approach better for you and your team." You could hear, "That sounds like exactly the right approach." Or you might hear, "I'm not sure how I'd change that," in which case you may have to ask again. And, of course, you open up the possibility that your dream client says, "Changing the start-up process will create a world of problems for us." The next question has to be "What could we do to get the outcome we need here?"

This is a good and effective approach, but because we are talking about a competitive displacement, we need to go even further. You have to give your prospective client a good reason to change, knowing that they are not going to fire their longtime partner without there being a compelling reason to do so. Let's look at making our case even more compelling.

HOW TO EXPAND THE DELTA

You increase the need to change by expanding the delta between your client's current results and the better results that are available to them. You do this by sharing the gaps in their performance, explaining how those gaps are growing, and sharing the implications of not taking action.

The ideas of Neil Rackham are hugely influential in this area. His concept of the "advance," the commitments that one gains along the way to a deal, was the catalyst for *The Lost Art of Closing*. Here we'll use another concept from Rackham's book *SPIN Selling* that is particularly potent in competitive displacements. That concept is the implications of not changing.

Even when the reasons to change are simple to understand and certain, it is still difficult for many people to change. In these cases, you must develop a more compelling case by dealing with the implications of not changing and retaining their current partner. This is a good practice in every deal, but you want to be careful not to overplay your hand. You can make your case with language that is so direct that you cause people to become defensive, making it more difficult for them to change and decreasing their desire to work with you. That said, it's important to create the largest delta between the current results your competitor is generating and the future results your dream client is capable of generating with your help. When your results far exceed your competitor's, you make it difficult for your client to retain them.

It might sound like, "I did some math on the fifteen percent increase in throughput and your current spend on overtime. Based on your numbers, that fifteen percent increase is worth just over $250,000, and the overtime savings is worth another $160,000 based on last year's numbers. The solution we are discussing increases your profitability by $410,000 in year one, minus the $225,000 you need to invest. That's positive $185,000 this year, and $410,000 next year. Over the next three years, this solution is worth just over one million dollars." The implications of not changing is now a loss of one million dollars on their bottom line, a compelling reason to take action now.

There are also soft costs, which are harder to quantify. Identifying the soft costs can help you build a greater delta, a bigger difference between the current state and the future state. The amount of time spent on rework is captured in overtime in the example I am using here, but it might also mean that your dream client is turning down other, more profitable work because they lack the bandwidth to take it. That is a soft cost that you can estimate to make your future state more compelling and the implications of not changing even greater. Maybe the rework is so frequent that they risk losing a key client. Or maybe they are turning over key staff members who are struggling with the required overtime hours.

I don't know your business or your client's business as well as you do, but I do know that there are always soft costs that companies overlook. Identifying and quantifying these soft costs is a way to expand the implications of not changing and to expand the delta between the results your competitor is generating and the better future results you are working on providing to them.

Just a word of caution here. You can expect your competitor to respond to this challenge by trying to match your solution, up their game, and start doing the things they should have been doing before you showed up. This can cause you to need to have a number of uncomfortable conversations. It's difficult to attack your competitor directly, pointing out that if they were unaware or unwilling to do these things before you showed up, they may also not know any number of other things they should. Instead, you are better off saying, "We look forward to being your partner on this project, and once we complete this we have three or four other ideas that we want to share with you." There is no guarantee that they won't give your competitor a chance to make the kind of improvement you just taught them was necessary, but it's my experience that even if they give them a couple weeks, once a prospect decides to change, they change.

DEVELOPING A SMALL OPPORTUNITY

Sometimes the way to begin a competitive displacement is to identify and pursue a small opportunity that shifts your status from "salesperson" to "partner," and shifts your company from one that is calling on your client to one that is already serving them and providing them with an invoice. This changes your status and gives you greater access to the people you need to create a displacement.

This book is focused on a pure takeaway, in which your competitor is removed and you take their place. You know how difficult it can be to remove a deeply entrenched strategic partner, even when they are struggling, and even when they are complacent. If you are being honest, you know some of your clients are exposed to being poached by your competitors, but they stay with you just to avoid the switching costs (it being too time-consuming to remove you and retrain a new partner). As much as I want you to take all of your competitor's business, there is a case for developing a small opportunity, the kind that gets you a foothold that you can expand over time.

In the very first sales training I ever attended, the fifty of us attendees were all given a role-play exercise in which we were to ask the client's regional manager for an order. The scenario included facts that made this an easy ask, as the client was struggling to have their orders filled by their current provider, they were falling behind on their work, and they needed help with some rather difficult-to-fill orders.

When I was called to the front of the room to do the role-play with the regional manager, I asked for all of the business. I said, "Your current partner is struggling to take care of you. We have the ability to provide you with the people you need. I'd like to give you a contract where we could be your primary provider." It was bold, audacious, and not what I had been instructed to do. But the reason I took this approach was because this was what my manager and I had been doing on a weekly basis, resulting in a tenfold increase in sales for our previously struggling branch.

The regional manager pushed back. I pushed harder. She pushed again. I pushed back, trying to "win" this battle of wills. She called for a break and pulled me aside and said, "I get what you are doing. I know it is working for you. But it doesn't always work, and sometimes the fastest way in is to just get an order so you have access." I was so wrapped around the axle trying to "win the deal" that I cut myself off from other possibilities. Later, the strategy she suggested helped me get orders, get access, and gain the trust to make a competitive displacement.

In a real deal I was pursuing, I had been calling on a large retailer's distribution center. Their partners were the two largest companies in the

United States. Neither of the partners was providing them with the results they needed, and they were open to "adding" another firm. They weren't even considering replacing one of these partners because they believed that if the two largest providers were incapable, no one else could do a better job.

I agreed to come on as a backup, simply filling the orders the other two firms left unfilled. That gave me access to the building and all the stakeholders. I started to show up daily on my way to my office to make sure we were producing results. That access allowed me to spend time with the stakeholders, developing relationships with all the people who had a say in who would be a partner. The second year, my company was a primary. The third year, we became the sole provider, using other agencies only when we needed to, and always as part of our overall program.

The key lesson here is that sometimes the right way to begin a displacement is with a single order.

Some companies use operating models under which they retain multiple providers. A tried-and-true strategy is the Champion-Challenger model where the client gives you, the Challenger, some percentage of the business as a hedge against the Champion. These companies find that they do well by having two providers competing for their business, one who gets the lion's share of the business (the Champion) and another who gets enough to be considered the Challenger. This approach is popular because it allows the company to shift a greater portion of their business to the Challenger should the Champion struggle, become complacent, or fail the client.

I am putting this strategy here for two reasons. First, if this is customary in your industry, you can win something less than a full competitive displacement and gain a new client. Eventually, if you are proactive enough and work on mindshare, you can become the Champion and crowd out your competitor, leaving them with the smaller portion of the business. The second reason I include this strategy is because I have seen salespeople successfully introduce it even in industries where it is not common. What differentiates this strategy from acquiring a small opportunity is that you ask for and gain a significant portion of the business. Instead of asking for a single order, you ask to pick up a percentage of the overall business, allowing the client a hedge against the current provider's possible failure.

I want to make it clear here that this strategy requires careful consideration. You cannot use this strategy if you are doing so only because you don't want to do the work it takes to create a full competitive displacement. This decision makes the most sense when it is difficult for one supplier to meet all the client's needs, or when the client's risk requires them to use multiple suppliers. If they must use two firms and you would not be cutting yourself off from a potential full displacement, this is a viable strategy. Just don't use it because you believe it is easier.

A FUNERAL FOR A FRIEND

It isn't easy to fire people with whom you have had long relationships. Your competitor has long-standing relationships with your dream client's company. They have a history of working together over time, and they have produced results in the past. They also likely have personal friendships, having spent time together, and having dealt with issues and challenges together. Your competitor knows the client's business in a way that makes it easier for the client to communicate with them, their history providing an understanding as to how things work.

The decision to replace these long-standing partners with you comes with switching costs. First, your dream client has to teach you their business. Even if you work with similar companies and in the same vertical, you know that every client has their own idiosyncrasies. Second, they have their own culture, their own way of communicating, their own preferences. They also have their own internal politics, people attempting to influence decision making—including decisions about who their partners are—in order to enhance their standing. Third, you are an unknown. You may or may not be able to produce the results you say you can. Others have tried and failed before you, and you sound a lot like those people, many of whom struggled greatly because they didn't understand how to work with their company.

Occasionally, you are lucky enough to come across a dream client that is so dissatisfied that they are ready and willing to remove their current partner. More often, however, they will extend that partner the same courtesy they would want from one of their clients should they struggle to get results—namely, a chance to make improvements. This makes competitive displacements a long game. It is one of professional, patient persistence. Make no mistake, it is difficult to fire people you have worked with for a long time, especially when you personally like them very much.

You make this more difficult when you speak poorly of your competitor, which can cause your client to feel the need to defend them. Remember, they chose your competitor, and at one point they did a good job. You must be careful about overplaying your hand when it comes to discussing your competitor's failings. In fact, it can be useful to give your client the rationale for letting them go by describing how much things have changed, how difficult the business is, how tough their business model is when it comes to producing the same result, and how you have a lot of respect for your competitor and the work they do. Someone has to do the difficult job of calling your competitor and letting them go, and you can make that easier by providing insights as to why they are not producing the result they need to—without saying a bad word about them.

Much of sales is made up of competitive displacements. The activity that begins that process is the creation of an opportunity, whether it be a small opportunity or a full displacement.

DO THIS NOW

---

1. Make a list of opportunities you are presently pursuing.

2. Write down their current state, the future state they need, and what they need to do to close the gap between the two.

3. Write down what you need to know to expand the delta, making the need to change more compelling and more valuable for your prospective client.

To download the worksheet that accompanies this chapter, go to www.eattheirlunch.training.

Chapter 7

BUILDING CONSENSUS HORIZONTALLY AND VERTICALLY

NO MATTER WHO YOU ENGAGE WITH DURING YOUR EARLY SALES interactions, you need to begin the process of building consensus around change—and around you as the right partner to help make that change. You first need to identify the stakeholders necessary to any change, and then you need to create a preference for you, your company, and your solution that is enough to gain you the right to displace your competitor.

IDENTIFYING THE STAKEHOLDERS

We very casually toss around the word "stakeholders" without ever defining the term and often without considering who these people really are. We use that word to mean everyone who will be affected by a decision to change, mostly limiting it to what we have historically defined as "decision makers" and "decision influencers." When we have someone helpful to our cause, we tend to get single-threaded, believing that our "coach," "champion," or "power sponsor" is enough to guide us to victory and a displacement. We are going to go deeper here to set up an understanding that provides a strategy to displace our competitor.

The CEO of the Problem: For a long time, you have been told you need to get to the C-suite. You've been taught to start as high up in the organization as possible, gain the support of the person with "authority," and then have that person push you down into the organization. Even though this sometimes works, it isn't very often true that you need the C-level executive, nor does what you might have to share always interest them (although you will do much better using the approach outlined in Part One of this book).

There is, however, someone who is responsible for making the very change you are trying to initiate. This is the person the CEO has charged with producing some result inside the company, and they trust that person to make decisions in their area of responsibility. That person is the CEO of the Problem. The CEO of the Problem is the highest-level person in charge of the kind of change that you would make in their organization. They have budgetary discretion, and even though they may need to get a signature from a level above theirs, they will have control over any change that is made.

The CEO isn't going to take a meeting that their CTO or CIO should be taking. The CEO hired and trusts these people to make good decisions because they have deeper subject matter expertise. The CTO or CIO in turn may have a director of IT that they trust to make certain decisions. Because they have delegated some authority to that individual, they may not take meetings with potential partners, leaving the decision to the person whom they charged with producing a certain set of results.

Let's be clear here who this person is: The person who cares most deeply about the results you produce and is charged with making sure they are delivered is the CEO of the Problem. It is important that you identify this person and that they are engaged as early as possible when it comes to displacing your competitor.

End Users: These are the stakeholders who use what you sell. They care deeply about Level 1 and Level 2 value.

Keep in mind that selling with Level 4 value doesn't mean prioritizing Level 4 value at the expense of the others. Level 4 includes the value created by the lower levels and allows you to create an opportunity by compelling change. There are people within your dream client's company who care very deeply about Level 1. In fact, if your competitor's product or service is producing subpar results, the end user stakeholder can be an excellent place to start a conversation, since understanding their challenges gives you an even more powerful case for change as you move up the org chart. It's also a good idea to have their support. (Remember: There isn't one right path when it comes to a deal, like always believing you must start at the top of the organization chart and work down.)

End user stakeholders are people you are going to help produce better results, and you are going to make their lives easier. Without their involvement in this process, you may come up with a solution that not only doesn't work, but is actively resisted by these stakeholders because you have stepped over and excluded them.

Ancillary Stakeholders: These stakeholders don't use what you sell, but it affects them in some way. They might represent the IT department or finance and accounting or human resources. They need you to consider their Level 2 needs.

You may not work directly with the accounting department of your dream client, but if you can't agree to give them the billing and reporting they need, you may find that they can make it difficult for you to win their business. Your competitor has already done the work to figure out how to serve them and you haven't. This means you look like more work for them.

It is increasingly the case that, because so many of our solutions require a technological component, even if it is only something like access to your portal, these ancillary stakeholders have a say in who they work with. These types of stakeholders tend to have outsized influence because their technical expertise allows them to make arguments that can be hard for other people to understand. They can also be underresourced, pushing back on any change initiative because their project board is already full.

These people need you to be easy to do business with, and you can't be that if you don't know what they need and why.

Management: These stakeholders need better results. They need their problems effectively addressed, and they need a partner in those results. They care most about Level 3 value, and much of the time, they care about Level 4 value. Level 3 value provides these stakeholders with a return on their investment, or what we referred to earlier as economic value. They also look for partners who are Level 4, those sales professionals who create strategic value and hold the role of trusted adviser. Management stakeholders look for better results now and better results in the future, as that is their charge. They also protect their people from failures at Levels 1 and 2. They remove the obstacles to performance and ensure that their team can execute. The kind of dissatisfaction that causes companies to change partners bubbles up to management—and from there, it sometimes makes it up to executive leadership.

Leadership: This is where your insights count the most. These stakeholders need Level 4 value. They need strategic thinking and actionable insights. They provide you with the ground cover you need from an executive sponsor, and they have the authority to sign a contract, binding their company to a deal. This is also the group of stakeholders that this book is designed to help you engage and win over.

Your insights, ideas, situational knowledge, and deep understanding of the issues that sit at the junction between your industry and your client's industry are what makes you someone interesting enough to meet. If you have deep knowledge and a point of view that provides the leadership stakeholders with something that helps them with a strategic initiative (or creates one for them), you can start to shift your position from that of salesperson to trusted counsel.

To get a clearer vision of the complicated map of stakeholders and the paths to consensus, we need to look through one more lens, the individual attributes of the individual stakeholders that provide us with choices.

ATTRIBUTES: MAKING THE SUBJECTIVE OBJECTIVE

To map your stakeholders and determine the choices available to you when building consensus, you need to make certain attributes that are subjective into something more objective.

I was in a workshop where a participant suggested that human beings make only rational, objective decisions based on evidence. I argued that the truth is quite the opposite, that people make emotional, irrational decisions. My statement caused further protestations to the contrary, with this gentleman insisting that I was incorrect. So I asked him to tell me about the spreadsheet and attributes he used to choose his spouse. He fumbled to find an argument, and then he replied, "She chose me!" I said, "So she made the irrational decision. Or did she use a spreadsheet?" Everyone laughed, but the man was unmoved.

At lunch, sandwiches were brought in for all the participants. As my "rational" friend walked by me, he held the sandwich in front of him like it was some kind of offering. He looked at me and said, "I am on the Paleo diet. I should not be eating this bread. But I really want this sandwich." He smiled at me, recognizing his decision was anything but rational or objective. I was positive that this was not the first or last decision of this kind that he would make.

All of the attributes here are subjective, even if we look at what evidence we can find to assess them. We will attempt to make these attributes look as if they are objective, knowing that the map is not the territory. We are only categorizing some of the attributes of the stakeholders, so we can ask better questions about what your choices are as you work through developing the relationships that will allow you to displace your competitor (though this section will no doubt help you with any deal, regardless of how you acquire the opportunity).

What you will discover as we start to score the stakeholders on these attributes is that you don't need to be exact, just directionally right. As you compare one stakeholder to others, you'll adjust the way you score each and gain a clearer picture of who can help you win their business and who is going to be an obstacle, while gaining perspective on some of your choices.

Perception of Value: How are you perceived by a stakeholder? What level of value do they believe you create and what level do they need you to create? Is there a gap, and what do you need to do to improve that perception?

There is a reason we start with the perception of value. You will have a very difficult time convincing someone who doesn't believe that you create greater value than their current provider that it makes sense to change to a company with which they've had no experience.

One of the questions I am most frequently asked about Level 4 value is whether you have to grow to that level or if you can start there. In a competitive displacement, you must start there. This is what I mean when I say you must enter the conversation from the right. You must come in with this higher level of value if you want to create a compelling case to change where there isn't one. End users care deeply about Level 1 value, and you may not need to do more than prove you can do a better job with your product or service to gain their support. But as you move up the organizational chart, you will need to create a greater level of value to win stakeholders, especially management and leadership.

Here you score your contacts on their perception of value using Levels 1 through 4 to give you an orienting generalization (remember, it's a map, not the territory).

Engagement Level: Is the stakeholder engaged or disengaged in the process? Will they meet with you? Will they share with you? Are they willing to collaborate?

To create and win an opportunity inside your competitor's client, you will need stakeholders who are engaged with you in the process of change. This means they will give you their time. It also means they will share information with you. They'll schedule meetings, make introductions, and say yes to the ten commitments in *The Lost Art of Closing*. Those commitments include the commitment of time, the commitment to explore, the commitment to change, the commitment to collaborate (which includes the exchange of information), the commitment to build consensus (which means providing access to other members of their team and stakeholders in other functions who will have a say in any change), the commitment to invest, the commitment to review your solution, and the commitment to resolve concerns.

Stakeholders who are engaged are very literally working through the process of change with you. Be very careful when you look at this attribute because it is easy to believe that higher engagement is better, which isn't always true. Proponents with high engagement are critical, and they will help you further your cause. But what about opponents, people who have a low perception of the value you create, prefer your competitor, and are highly engaged in the process? As you will soon discover, the combination of engaged and opposed makes someone an opponent.

You can score a contact from 1 to 5, with 1 representing "very disengaged," 5 "very engaged," and the numbers in between standing for some partial level of engagement. While it can seem beneficial to have a stakeholder who is very engaged, a person with a 5 on engagement (highly engaged) with a 1 on preference (meaning they support your competitor) makes for a difficult stakeholder. You are really looking for the difference between individuals as much as their individual score. Pick a number, then revise it when you realize the difference between stakeholders.

Compelled to Change: The status quo is a very difficult foe. No matter how strong your case for change, there are stakeholders who will resist or refuse any initiative to change. Creating and capturing an opportunity requires you to win hearts and minds. There will be others, however, who are highly motivated. These stakeholders are instrumental in creating opportunities and making real change.

What you are looking for here is a way to determine who wants this change enough that they are willing to do the work inside their company. You want to find the people who need things to be better than they are. I know there are models that suggest that there is a single person who can drive change in their organization, with monikers like "coach," "champion," "sponsor," "power sponsor," or my friends at CEB Gartner's "mobilizer," from their book *The Challenger Customer*. All of these are fine, but we need to go further. We need to look at where all the stakeholders line up here.

People who are highly compelled to change are more susceptible to removing their current provider. The more compelled they are, the more helpful they tend to be in a displacement. But the opposite is also true. The less compelling they find the prospect of change, the more likely they are to work against it. To understand the dynamics and your choices, you must look at the scores in multiple attributes, as a single attribute tells you only a small part of the story. Someone may be highly compelled to change, highly engaged, but prefer a company other than yours. Maybe they've done business with them in the past, and they love the idea of firing their current partner but will actively work against you and your company. Therefore, you can't allow one attribute to dominate your thinking here.

You can use the same scoring here, starting with 1 being completely resistant to any change and 5 being so compelled to change that they will absolutely vote to change no matter what, and 3 being neutral.

Authority: Another factor you must consider when analyzing your stakeholder map is how much authority an individual has, as well as their willingness to use it. You need these folks, especially when they are leadership stakeholders, to provide support for your opportunity and help you protect opportunities from internal and external threats.

You may have heard of the BANT method for qualifying prospective clients, wherein you gauge an opportunity based on a contact confirming their Budget, Authority, Needs, and Time. This method for qualifying prospects has been in use for as long as I can remember. But there are too many cases where a prospective client doesn't have a budget (the B in BANT) but can invest when there is a compelling reason to do so. There are also companies and people who have needs (N) they have not yet recognized, as you learned in Part One of this book. For many of our prospective clients, changing in April is just as good as changing in March. Even though sooner is better than later for you, time (T) doesn't always count for much for your clients.

This leaves us with the A in BANT: authority. The idea of authority presupposes that there is a single individual with the power to decide and bind the company to a deal. It is true that there will be a single person who signs a contract, but that person will not likely make the decision themselves. Nowadays, decisions are made more democratically, with leaders preferring consensus over command and control. They want their people to bring their initiative and resourcefulness to solving their problems, and they want their buy-in and ownership of the execution of any decision to change.

That said, you still need executive support, and you'll have to ask who will sign any agreement, who will be on the buying committee, and how the decision will be made. You also must score people on how much formal authority they have within the organization. You make a displacement unlikely when you don't include the people with the authority to say yes to moving forward with you when they are signing the contract and the check.

The CEO of your dream client's company is a 5 when it comes to authority. But the CEO of the Problem may also be a 5, having the final decision over whether they will change providers, what the solution will look like, and who will be their future partner.

Before you think about scoring the other stakeholders, it's good to consider the next section on influence. Influence is another form of authority and power. It isn't always easy to see unless you are paying careful attention. Why is it that there are stakeholders with no formal authority but who have outsized power? Let's look at influence.

Influence: Influence is similar to authority, except that it is invisible. It has nothing to do with titles, and you can't see it on an org chart or on LinkedIn profiles. Influence is based on the weight some individual carries as it concerns what you sell and as it concerns change. This attribute determines whom people look to to guide their thinking and their beliefs.

There are people in every company with the kind of subject matter expertise that makes them a 5 when it comes to influence. You can identify these people in meetings because they ask a lot of questions and are vocal about what they want. You can also identify people with influence because their peers ask them questions, leaning on their subject matter expertise to understand something or decide what their choices might be. But while some people with influence make themselves known to you, others can be harder to uncover. They sit quietly, saying nothing, never tipping their hand. But behind the scenes, they work to make their preferences known, and are taken seriously when they do. One way to flush out these stakeholders is to ask them to share their thoughts in meetings, causing them to have to say something. You might also have to ask an engaged stakeholder who prefers to give you a better read on that individual, so you know how best to engage them.

Influencers can be powerful allies, or they can be formidable opponents. A quiet influencer may undermine you behind the scenes, or you can have a very vocal influencer who makes their opposition to you and your company known—even when you are sitting in the room with them. I once had an influencer with outsized power tell me that my company's price was too high, that we were not a good partner, and that she was going to go with a company with a much lower price, believing there was no way we could create enough value to command the investment we asked for. She worked tirelessly to ensure that another company got her business. It was only after she left that her company hired us to do the work the way we had proposed.

Influence is one of the factors you must consider carefully. Someone with no formal authority can have massive influence. You risk overlooking this person because you don't see the outward appearances of power, not recognizing that they have the most power in the room, even more than someone with formal authority.

In another deal I was involved with, a stakeholder was so unhappy and complained so frequently and so loudly that it was clear her influence was greater than the rest of her peers'. Her division of the company also spent more than the other divisions. Although she lacked a great deal of formal authority, winning her support was enough to ensure that my little company beat one of the largest firms in the world for her business. Because we recognized her influence and spent time with her while they ignored her needs (something that built the case for change), we took their business from them.

A score of 5 is high influence and a score of 1 is no influence. The other scores will reveal themselves to you as you compare one stakeholder to another. Invariably someone will say, "If Joe is a 4 when it comes to influence, then Jane is 5." If you want the best hedge against mistakes when it comes to influence, then you will treat everyone from the janitor to the CEO with respect and assume they have more influence than you can see. Your mom told you this, and she was correct then, as she is now.

Preference: This isn't an easy factor to score, but, like all the rest, it is critical. This factor is a measurement of who the stakeholder prefers to work with now.

Some stakeholders will make it very clear that they want to work with you by telling you as much. That makes a score of 5 an accurate assessment. There are others who will tell you, in word or deed, that they prefer someone else. And some will give you no clue. To uncover their preference, you need to ask them directly or ask other stakeholders who are compelled to change, engaged, and have a preference for you.

Remember that any one of these factors by itself provides only a very small piece of the map. Someone can prefer you while having no influence and no authority. You can also have someone with a strong preference for your competitor who has high influence and authority. They may work to protect their preferred partner from being displaced, and you should expect this to be the case. Maybe they perceive their existing provider to be a Level 4 value provider. Once you have scored your stakeholders on these attributes, you can see another picture, one you may not have seen before.

BUILDING CONSENSUS WORKSHEET

Stakeholder	Title	Role	Present Level of Value	Goal Level of Value	Preference	Engagement	Compelling Reason to Change	Authority	Influence
Jane Jones	VP	CEO of the Problem	Level 1	Level 3	5	4	1	5	5
John Johnson	Director		Level 3	Level 4	4	4	4	2	4
Tom McCarthy	IT		Level 3	Level 3	3	3	3	2	3
Steve Anand	Operations Manager		Level 2	Level 3	2	3	2	3	3
Brian Harris	Operations Lead		Level 1	Level 3	1	5	1	3	5
Sue Smith	CFO		Level 1	Level 3	3	3	3	3	3

ALLIES, OBSTACLES, AND OPPONENTS

Once you have scored all potential stakeholders, let's sort them into five types based on their attributes so you can recognize them and make good decisions about your strategy to build consensus.

Allies: Allies prefer you and your solution over their present provider. They are highly engaged in the process, and they have a large amount of influence as it pertains to this opportunity. They are also highly compelled to change.

As a general strategy, you may want to consider identifying as many allies as possible as early in the process as possible. This is a good place to start building consensus around a displacement, because as you get deeper into the process you build momentum and make an initiative to change providers more difficult to stop. Ask the question, "Who will be supportive of the kind of change we are recommending here and when can we bring them into this conversation?"

Potential Allies: Potential allies are neutral when it comes to changing their partner and neutral when it comes to engagement with the process. They may be in meetings only because an ally asked them to be there. But they can potentially be influenced. They have some influence, and they may have some need to change, but they aren't yet compelled to act.

You are going to talk to your allies about potential allies. You will ask for help identifying who is most likely to support bringing you in as a partner and whose support you can win. You may want to avoid bringing in people who are not friendly to the idea of releasing your competitor until later in the process.

Neutral: There are some stakeholders who are neutral across the board. They tend to be ancillary stakeholders who gain or lose nothing when it comes to hiring you and removing your competitor. Still, they may be necessary, and increasing their ranking in any of these factors is helpful. You also want to avoid anything that increases their preference for your competitor or causes them to resist changing.

Obstacles: Obstacles do not prefer you and may prefer your competitor. They are not easily engaged in this process, have high influence, and are not compelled to change. There are times when you must bring these people into the sales conversation earlier than you want. They tend to be subject matter experts and have a lot of knowledge and experience. If you know they prefer your competitor, you may want to leave them out of the conversation until you have a strong firewall of support.

Opponents: Opponents prefer someone else and their solution, are engaged in the process, have very high influence, and either are not compelled to change or are compelled but prefer someone other than you to replace their current provider. These are the people who will actively work against you.

You can deal with obstacles and opponents in one of two ways. The first, which is my preferred approach, is to isolate them by avoiding bringing them into the process for as long as possible and building as much consensus as possible first. By the time you engage with them, you have so much momentum that they lack the power to stop a displacement. The risk with this approach is that their influence is so high and their relationships so deep that lacking their support causes others to defect.

The second approach is to engage them earlier in the process. Bringing them in early allows them to surface their issues and the reasons why they oppose removing your competitor or more generally resist change. This strategy tends to work best when you have a good deal of support from an executive sponsor who is highly compelled to change with the power to overrule an opponent. But you need to be careful here. More and more leaders are seeking consensus (green values) around important decisions, and some will struggle with the idea of using force (red values) to get things done. Leaving key people out of the process and making them feel excluded can give them the moral high ground and allow them to argue that their voice wasn't heard.

When it comes to building consensus within your client, you need to ask yourself the following questions:

- When does it make sense to bring in additional stakeholders?
- Who is likely to support this initiative or idea?

- Is there a way to win the support of the people who are not yet compelled to change?
- How do we deal with obstacles whose engagement might just as easily cause us problems as benefit us?
- When do we engage those who oppose changing partners?

BUILDING CONSENSUS WORKSHEET: IDENTIFYING ROLES

Stakeholder	Title	Role	Present Level of Value	Goal Level of Value	Preference	Engagement	Compelling Reason to Change	Authority	Influence
Jane Jones	VP	CEO of the Problem	Level 1	Level 3	5	4	1	5	5
John Johnson	Director	Ally	Level 3	Level 4	4	4	4	2	4
Tom McCarthy	IT	Neutral	Level 3	Level 3	3	3	3	2	3
Steve Anand	Operation Manager	Obstacle	Level 2	Level 3	2	3	2	3	3
Brian Harris	Operation Lead	Opponent	Level 1	Level 3	1	5	1	3	5
Sue Smith	CFO	Potential Ally	Level 1	Level 3	3	3	3	3	3

As you ask and answer these questions you want to make certain that you are considering the sequence. In what order does it make sense to have these conversations?

Let me summarize this entire chapter in a way that makes it easier to understand and gives you something you can use right now. To build consensus:

1. Identify the attributes of the various contacts you have at the client organization.

2. Based on their attributes, categorize them as allies, potential allies, neutral, obstacles, or opponents.

3. Work on increasing the engagement and preference you have from the CEO of the Problem, allies, and potential allies.

4. Determine when it is necessary to engage obstacles and how you will address their concerns. Deal with obstacles with higher influence and authority first.

5. Determine your strategy for when you will engage with opponents and how.

There are people who have to know you and who must believe that they need to change. They also must believe that you are the right partner. First you build consensus that change is necessary, and then you build consensus that you are the right partner. When you have consensus, the competitive displacement becomes all but inevitable.

DO THIS NOW

1. Make a list of stakeholders inside a client with whom you are engaged in the sales process now.

2. Score each one on the following attributes: preference, compelled to change, engagement, authority, influence, and their perception of value you create.

3. Based on the scores you assign them, sort the stakeholders into allies, potential allies, obstacles, neutral, and opponents.

To download the worksheet that accompanies this chapter, go to www.eattheirlunch.training.

Chapter 8

FINDING A PATH TO A DEAL

THERE ARE TWO MAJOR TYPES OF CHALLENGES YOU MAY EN-
counter when finding a path to an agreement. The first type is internal
challenges within your dream client's company, when the various stakeholders may not all be on the same page. The second type is the mistakes
we often make when we believe our goal is to displace a competitor. Let's
start by examining the internal challenges.

INTERNAL CHALLENGES

Your Stakeholders Disagree on the Problem: Sometimes your client's internal stakeholders don't agree that there is a problem or that the problem
is worth solving. Some stakeholders believe their issues require a new solution and a new strategic partner, while others may not think those same
problems are worth solving at all, being much more comfortable with the
status quo than some of their peers.

You see this in the attributes we discussed above. The stakeholders
who are compelled to change believe the problem is one worth the devo-
tion of their time, energy, resources, and money. Those opposed find the
opposite to be true. Resistance from some doesn't mean there is no path to

a deal. It suggests that you need to decide whether you can prevail over the opposition of those who are not compelled to change, or whether you—or someone from their team—can convince them that they need to do something different.

Building consensus is an art, not a science. You make decisions based on the situation, what you know, and what you believe your courses of action to be. I've seen stakeholders so removed from the severity of their problem that, when shown the facts, they quickly understood the need to change. Others have denied all evidence, believing that the problem wasn't as bad as it was made out to be, stubbornly refusing to take action. Sometimes senior management holds this position to their detriment. One company I worked with refused to change despite the overwhelming evidence I presented to them. For two years I told them their strategy was untenable and that they would lose clients. The senior leaders believed me only when they actually started to lose clients.

When there is an internal disagreement as to the problem, you must decide whether to find a path that avoids those who are resistant to changing, to work on winning their hearts and minds, or whether you can make a power play and find someone who overrules the opposition. This last strategy can be dangerous, as it can open you up to creating a group of people who will resist executing the new strategy and work to create failures that they can blame on you and you alone. A critical mass of people who are opposed to change can make a path to a deal difficult. Even when the stakeholders agree on the problem, they may have other areas of disagreement.

Your Stakeholders Disagree on the Solution: The stakeholders within your dream client who agree on the problem may disagree on what the right solution is. They may have conflicting ideas about what they should do, if anything.

Those who are compelled to change and who support you believe that changing is the right solution. Those people who prefer their existing supplier think the correct answer is to work with their current provider to make improvements. You may also find that some stakeholders have another horse in the race, bringing in another potential partner with a different solution. One of the challenges that may come on the back of creating a compelling case for change is that it can cause your dream client to look at options outside of you and your company, even initiating an RFP.

One of the reasons it is critical that you build consensus is that by spending time with the right stakeholders—and in the proper sequences—you create support for you, your company, and your solution. Later we will explore why the sequence of meetings with stakeholders can make a difference in the result, but ultimately you are trying to build sufficient support for your solution early enough that it can withstand any threats that appear later in the process.

You need to build consensus around the problem, the solution, and finally the process, often the most difficult of the three. Let's look at stakeholders who disagree with the process.

Your Stakeholders Disagree on the Process: It's problematic enough that you have stakeholders who disagree on the problem and whether it needs to be dealt with now—or at all. It's also difficult when they aren't on the same page with respect to the solution. But these challenges are relatively straightforward. You run into real difficulties when your prospective clients can't agree about the process of changing, which is made more difficult in a competitive displacement, when you've initiated the case for change and disrupted the status quo.

In a competitive displacement, you are a subversive force. You are trying to change the established way people are doing things, which includes working with the current provider. You aren't responding to a request for a proposal, a formal process that already exists and presumes the intention of exploring the change to a new partner. You may not even be working with a group of people who have ever discussed what it would take for them to change from their current partner.

Because of this, you must help your contacts identify the process by asking them who needs to be part of the conversation, who needs to be part of any group that makes the decision to change, who will be affected by this decision, and when it's best to engage them.

Some sales leaders place a heavy emphasis on following a fixed sales process, with the belief that structure leads to better outcomes. I, on the other hand, have always been sales process agnostic, believing that a sales process is necessary but not sufficient to sell well, mostly because I have spent most of my life executing competitive displacements. There was never a fixed process that marked out all the required conversations and outcomes, and in these situations the process has always been nonlinear. The same is true as it pertains to the buying process or buyer's journey, that is, the stages that buyers go through on their way to making a decision. Attempting to create and follow a one-size-fits-all map ignores the differences from one business to the next. These maps also make the damaging assumption that everyone in the buying organization is at the same stage of the process at the same time, which is almost never true (as you now know from having mapped out their attributes).

You are not likely to find that your sales process addresses any of these problems. But that doesn't mean you shouldn't help your prospective clients overcome these challenges and make the changes necessary to produce the results they need now. When most people see this framework, they recognize the three problems above as issues that have killed deals they believed they were positioned to win. As the one doing the displacing, your awareness of these challenges and ability to recognize them provides you with an opportunity to address them.

WHEN YOU ARE YOUR OWN WORST ENEMY

Sometimes, the problems you have in building consensus are of your own making.

Moving Forward Without the Necessary Stakeholders: The first and most dangerous mistake you can make when consensus is necessary is trying to move forward without having done all the necessary work. Trying to push a deal forward without bringing in all the people who need to say yes to your deal will cause them to pull on the reins, slow things down, resist the change, and eventually try their best to kill the initiative. Even though consensus is difficult under the best of conditions, trying to avoid it can destroy your opportunity to win. Why, then, do so many salespeople try to avoid this work?

One of the reasons salespeople avoid identifying and engaging with every necessary stakeholder is their fear of alienating their primary contact. You might believe that the one critical relationship you have with a stakeholder who is highly engaged is enough to win the deal. You will then have to face reality when the same stakeholder is the one to tell you that "the company has decided to go in another direction." "The company," in this case, refers to the stakeholders who were left out of the process altogether. We sometimes fear the wrong danger. The fear of bringing in additional parties isn't our greatest threat; leaving them out of the process is the real danger.

The desire to have the deal *now* is another reason why salespeople try to move forward without the people who make up the buying committee, formal or informal. They want to rush the process because they have goals to meet, and a deal now is better than a deal later. You need to recognize that your sales process is not the buyer's process, and no matter how well you try to align them, things will get misaligned as soon as human beings enter the picture. When your sales process requires you to target your dream clients, qualify them, do good discovery work, then present your solution, that is what you believe to be the right process. What the process doesn't tell you is that there are seven people involved in the decision, and four of them have no idea that anyone is considering a change.

You might also try jamming through a deal without the necessary support because you have no strategy for dealing with opponents, those stakeholders who will work against you and the change you want to make—and who may be highly supportive of the competitor you are working to displace. The fact that you avoid an opponent doesn't in any way lessen their influence on whether or not their company moves forward with you. The decision to engage or avoid a stakeholder is a difficult one. You will need to look at your choices and choose the strategy you believe benefits you. This book is about competitive displacements, one of the more difficult outcomes to achieve in sales. Achieving this goal naturally requires more of you, including engaging with people who don't agree with you, who are working to protect their turf, and who are going to oppose you.

Committing to a Single Strategy: When salespeople are single-threaded (working with a single contact and believing that is all that is necessary), they often commit to one course of action. By committing to their first idea, they don't leave themselves open to other possibilities as they emerge.

When you start thinking vertically and horizontally, you begin to see where multiple stakeholders will be involved in the process and affected by any decision to change, and you need to adapt your strategy to meet their specific needs. You must think about how you can help them along the decision path. Your primary contact may have given you their time, explored change, decided they have a compelling reason to do something different, committed to change, and collaborated with you in building the right solution. Now you need to consider where the rest of the organization is as it pertains to this change. Some of the stakeholders you need may not even be at the stage where they are ready to explore the need to change, let alone commit to that change.

What is the value proposition for the people who will be affected by a decision to change? What is your process for engaging with them to help them agree to the change?

Not Exploring the Sequence of Events: When you start thinking about building the consensus necessary to fire your competitor and replace them with you and your solution, you recognize that the sequence in which you decide to do things can matter a great deal. If your experience demonstrates that you will need representatives from your prospective client's IT department, you must decide when to bring them into the process. Does it serve you better to bring them in early, helping them to understand why changing to you from your competitor is essential, making them part of the early discussions? Or are you better served when you wait until you have the support of an executive leader who can force them to do whatever is necessary to make the change?

If you have read my previous work, you know that I don't believe there are right or wrong answers. You don't want to limit your possibilities. Sales is a complex, dynamic, nonlinear human interaction, with too many variables for there to be one right answer for all situations. Instead, you need to be thoughtful and strategic about making the best possible decision based on the information you have and your experiences.

I have seen companies take the unconventional strategy of first approaching the purchasing department to create an opportunity, providing them with the value proposition of investing more to get results, explaining the soft costs they were incurring, and asking for their help in teaching the rest of the organization how to understand their real costs. This bold approach is often successful, but they would never have considered it if they believed that purchasing could only ever be an obstacle.

———

We'll investigate how to make decisions around sequencing your meetings later in this chapter. For now, you need to know that you must make decisions about the strategy to bring other stakeholders into the process, and in what order.

HOW TO BUILD CONSENSUS

Determining the Outcomes You Need

Determining the outcomes you need to build consensus can be tricky. Let me give you an example. You are calling on your dream client and engage a person you recognize as being the CEO of the Problem, the person most concerned with producing better results. He gives you a deep understanding of his challenge and explains what he believes he needs to be able to achieve his goals. Because you are a peer and a trusted adviser type of salesperson, you ask the question "Who will be impacted by a decision to change here, and who will be involved in a decision of this magnitude?" Your CEO of the Problem tells you there are five people who get to weigh in on this decision: the head of operations, the head of IT, the senior floor supervisor, and their number-two person. Because you are smart, you ask, "Can you share with me a little about each one of them, what they're going to need to support this, and what their concerns might be, if they have any?"

Your CEO of the Problem gives you the lay of the land. The head of operations needs to know that anything you do together doesn't disrupt her ability to serve her clients. They can't experience an interruption. The head of IT needs to be certain that whatever you do can be integrated into their ERP software. The senior floor supervisor and their number-two person will be opposed to change and want to retain their current partner. They are paid for performance, and they've not done well for a while, but they don't want to do anything different.

You may discover all of this in the course of one meeting or over five meetings with different people. The point here is to understand the outcomes you need to deliver for each stakeholder. In this case, you need to resolve the head of operations' concern about her ability to run production while you change over to whatever you sell. You need someone from your technical team to convince the head of IT that you can integrate what you are doing into their ERP. Somehow, you'll also have to convince the senior floor supervisor and their peer that they need to change—and that you will be an even better partner for them than their current partner. Eliciting what different people need provides you with the opportunity to take the necessary actions to win their support.

Sequencing and Deciding When to Engage Stakeholders

Deciding when to bring in stakeholders is very important but can be tricky. You can follow one of three strategies here. None of these strategies are mutually exclusive; you can employ a number of these at the same time, the main goal being to avoid obstacles early on and gain enough support to defend the need to change.

The first strategy is to identify early on the people who will be supportive of hiring you to replace their current provider and to build a critical mass of support before dealing with any obstacles. By creating a foundation of support, you can make it more difficult for those opposed to your effort to halt your progress, it being too late for them to make their case once support reaches critical mass. This strategy works most of the time, but it can backfire when a highly influential stakeholder works behind the scenes to stop your competitive displacement. There is almost always someone influential at the client organization with a deep relationship with your competitor who will work to retain them. In the hypothetical above, you might decide to tackle the head of operations and IT before tackling the senior supervisor. By building support with the three key stakeholders, you make it more difficult for the supervisor and their number two to stop the initiative.

The second strategy is to acquire executive sponsorship early in the process to ensure that you have ground cover to protect you from any resistance. By acquiring executive-level support early in the process, you have some protection against a decision to retain your competitor. Let's stick with the hypothetical above. Let's say you created an opportunity with the senior supervisor and their team instead of the higher-level stakeholders. They inform you that the heads of operations and IT will oppose any change, as they have a deep relationship with your competitor (a scenario that is just as likely to be true). You may decide to avoid the heads of operations and IT until you have the CEO of the Problem's support—or maybe the support one level up from them.

The third strategy is to bring people who are not compelled to change and who have high influence into the process in the early discovery meetings. By bringing them into the conversation early, you surface their resistance and deal with those issues and concerns. I have personally had experiences in displacing competitors where it was necessary to bring the obstacles into the process early and win their support to replace a competitor. Including them in the process allowed other stakeholders and a member of the executive leadership team to work on flipping them from "opposed" to "standing down."

Bringing in opponents early is an important possibility to consider as it pertains to building consensus and managing change. Consensus does not mean you need a unanimous decision. It means that you have enough support to change and that those who oppose you stand down and do what is best for the company—even when it doesn't serve them or creates some new challenges for them. It can be helpful to have these conversations early in the process. You say, "Some people on your team may have to be willing to stand down and do what is best for the company to produce the new results you need. Whose help will we need in convincing them to move forward and how do we mitigate the new challenges this creates?"

DEALING WITH OBSTACLES

Deciding to Engage or Avoid Obstacles

Some opponents need to be engaged in the process or you risk losing the opportunity. Others are better avoided, at least until they no longer pose a threat.

When given the choice of engaging obstacles and opponents or avoiding them altogether, I tend to engage. I believe I can help people move to a place where they will agree to change. That doesn't mean this is always the right choice. I have had the unfortunate experience of engaging with an opponent to the change I was trying to make early in the process, where I inadvertently provided them with the ammunition they needed to work behind the scenes to destroy any possibility of change. Once I showed them my solution, they were able to go to my competitor and make the changes necessary to retain their current partner. It was a choice that I made, and in that case, it cost me a deal.

There are cases in which it can make sense to avoid an opponent. If you know that an opponent's support for your competitor is so strong there is no way they will ever agree to a decision to change, arming them with your solution may provide them with what they need to work against you. You might also choose to avoid a vocal opponent with low influence when you are confident they can do no harm. There are some people who go through every change kicking and screaming. Like the boy who cried wolf, they lose any real influence, having opposed every change their company ever proposed.

The choices you make along the path of building consensus can speed displacement, or they can cause resistance to the very idea of changing. Taking your dream client from your competitor requires that you build consensus.

Mitigating the Challenges

It is always better to minimize the challenges that cause some stakeholders to oppose your initiative than it is to leave them entirely out of the process. Working with your team and the client's team to come up with ideas to gain support improves relationships and compliance. One of the reasons you want to consider engaging your opponents is that you need to do what you can to mitigate any challenges you create for them. Some of these may be easily resolved, while others can be difficult. If your dream client needs to shift the date that you might begin implementing a solution, this can be a relatively easy challenge to mitigate. It might also be easy to mitigate the challenge of providing additional resources, like training or support. These constraints can be overcome with some effort and creativity.

However, if someone opposes hiring you because they have a close relationship with your competitor, the factor you are trying to improve is their preference. It can be challenging to flip someone from complete support for your competitor to supporting you. If they don't believe that change is necessary, you may be able to improve their willingness to support change by helping them understand what is at stake and by having their peers help them understand why it is necessary. Even when they believe change is necessary, it's difficult to increase your preference when the relationship with your competitor is the real obstacle. This can take a lot of time and effort.

Sometimes the challenge a stakeholder has in supporting change isn't so much that they are in love with your competitor but that your solution causes them problems. Maybe it changes their process. Perhaps it means that they'll lose members of their team. It might require that they do more work at a time when they are already stretched and lack the resources they need. By engaging with stakeholders who are obstacles, you get the chance to uncover these challenges—and you get the opportunity to mitigate them. You can't solve a problem without knowing what it is. Your role in mitigating these challenges requires that you learn what the obstacle is, that you work to resolve it, and that you work with the rest of your dream client's team to come up with a solution that works. You may not get an obstacle's full support for the change, but you may move them to a place where they can "stand down."

Do You Have the Commitments You Need?

You need to control the process as much as is humanly possible. This doesn't mean that you slavishly follow a fixed, predetermined process. Nor does it mean that you allow the client to determine the best course forward. Instead, it means you adapt to their organizational needs while guiding them to make the necessary commitments to achieve their desired outcomes. It is a mistake to believe that your client has a well-considered plan for having the conversation they need to have around changing partners. In *The Lost Art of Closing* I wrote about the ten commitments necessary to win sales: time, explore, change, collaborate, build consensus, invest, review, resolve concerns, decide, and execute. The three commitments that concern us here are the commitments to collaborate, build consensus, and resolve concerns (even though all of them are necessary).

You need to gain the commitment to collaborate so you can create a solution that is better than your competitor's, so you can ensure that it includes the stakeholders you need to support change. This commitment and the commitment to build consensus are often intertwined. While you are collaborating, you are developing consensus and vice versa.

One of the ways you build consensus is by resolving the concerns of the stakeholders who may not support you because they are afraid that things are not going to be better. They may be worried that replacing a partner who knows the business with someone untried and untested puts the company at risk. They may have concerns that your approach won't work or that you won't be there to support them through the process. Whatever their issues, without eliciting and dispatching them efficiently, it is difficult for a stakeholder who has concerns to support hiring you.

You must know what commitments you need and from whom. Without the right commitments, consensus is difficult. Do you know what we need from each stakeholder? Do you have a strategy for developing consensus?

This whole chapter is a strategy for wiring the building. It's about developing the understanding, the relationships, and a plan for engaging in this work. The basic idea you need to execute is to answer the questions we covered:

- "Whom do we need to engage?"
- "What do we need to gain their support?"
- "In what order do we have these meetings?"
- "What is the outcome of those meetings?"

What you will find as you map out a strategy—and especially if you do so with a team of smart people—is that there are multiple strategies available to you. You'll discover that you can start with the chief marketing officer and ask them to speak to the controller to help gain their support around the investment your dream client needs to make to improve what they are doing, an investment that is slightly higher than their current provider. You might also identify a strategy that includes icing out the controller until you have more support, and until you can produce an ROI analysis that proves your higher price lowers costs.

What is important to note when you're building consensus is that you don't have only one path to consensus. You want multiple ways to a deal, so you never hit a dead end. When things don't work as expected, you can always choose another route.

Have We Worked to Make It Easier for Opponents to Stand Down?

When someone will be negatively affected by a change you need to make to help your dream client produce better results, you can sometimes gain their support by mitigating the challenge you present. The starting point is gaining an understanding of how what you do causes problems.

If you are reading this book or listening to it on audio, then you have no doubt done the work of making changes to gain a stakeholder's support. In one deal I led, a stakeholder needed support for the service that we offered in three locations. We had built-in support for only one of those locations to make the solution cost effective. To win over two stakeholders we had to agree to give them minimal support at their shift start, and they had to decide to share that resource. That was enough to mitigate their challenge with the solution and remove their resistance.

In another scenario, to mitigate concerns from one department, one of my companies had to agree to use the client's vendor for a particular service—even though it was inferior and more expensive than the service we used. The result of using their service was no different, but it was necessary to mitigate one stakeholder's concern about the quality of the results. Changing to their vendor wasn't worth losing a deal over, so we did what we needed to do to mitigate their concern.

That said, you will not always be able to mitigate every stakeholder's concern, and it isn't always possible to make changes that might gain someone's support without putting the solution and the outcomes you are creating at risk.

You will not always be able to gain the support of every stakeholder yourself. In some cases, you will need someone from your dream client's team to win their support—or to ask them not to oppose the change. If you want someone to intervene to gain support or ask an opponent to stand down, you will have to ask directly. You'll need to say, "Can I ask you to ask Tom in IT to support the change we are trying to make or at least not to oppose it? I am afraid if he is obstinate here and continues to oppose what we are doing we'll have trouble moving this forward."

One of the best ways to accomplish this was mentioned earlier, namely gaining executive support. When you are removing a current supplier and changing things to produce a better result, you will occasionally need to have more challenging conversations.

There is always a path to a deal, even if it is a difficult path to identify—and a challenging one to take.

DO THIS NOW

1. Make a list of contacts within a prospective client you are pursuing now.

2. Identify the buying committee and the CEO of the Problem.

3. Make a list of outcomes you need in order to ensure that the buying committee chooses you.

4. Make a list of meetings you need to have with these contacts and in what order.

To download the worksheet that accompanies this chapter, go to www.eattheirlunch.training.

PART 3

WINNING WITH
THE INTANGIBLES

Much of the preference that leads to a displacement is made up of intangibles, those things that can't easily be measured and have little to do with your product, your service, or even your company. This section will help you build these intangibles into a competitive advantage and make you someone worth leaving an existing partner for.

Chapter 9

CREATING A PREFERENCE

WE OFTEN FORGET THAT THE ACT OF SELLING IS ABOUT CREAT-
ing a preference to work with us instead of our competitor. Nowhere is this
more essential than in a competitive displacement, since that is the single
desired outcome. Mindshare equals wallet share, and the intangibles are a
large part of what creates that preference. In this chapter, you will learn
how to make the intangibles your competitive advantage.

YOUR CLIENT IS BUYING YOU

We have to address something here that is rarely spoken of and not given
the consideration it deserves. You are now the most significant part of the
value proposition. The fact that you are one of the primary factors your
client considers may come as a surprise, and this may be the first time
anyone has made you aware of this fact. Whether or not you want to believe this, the fact is that your performance gets weighted heavily in a decision to change.

There is a very high likelihood that your company's slide deck opens
up with a picture of your headquarters, the organizational chart for your
leadership team, a list of your locations, and a slide that shows all the logos

of the big, well-recognized clients your company serves. All of this is offered to prove that you are a credible company with whom your prospect should want to work. These slides are designed to answer the question "Why should I work with your company?"

After your company history, your slide deck likely goes into your products and solutions. If the product alone were the value proposition, then you could just be an order-taker and reach your goals. If your product were so compelling that your clients would line up to buy it, your prospective clients wouldn't treat it—and you—like a commodity. The features and benefits would be so overwhelmingly important that your potential clients would change their operations to acquire that product. If this is not true for you, if your clients don't switch the minute you show them your products, then your product is not the value proposition.

So your company, with its storied history and recognized industry leaders, isn't enough to compel your dream client to remove your competitor, their long-serving partner. Your products and solutions are also impotent when it comes to producing this result, being wholly inadequate to create an answer to the question "Why should I change what I am doing now?" That means the real value lies somewhere else, that a higher level of value is necessary to create the case for change. Here we return to the four levels of value that opened this book on displacing your competitor and eating their lunch.

Selling at the first level of value makes you a pure commodity, and commodities don't create a case for change. The second level provides a better experience through service and support, but unless your competitor is so awful that it is causing severe damage to your dream client's results, it is table stakes. For a long time, we have sold at the third level of value, Level 3. But because you and I can both produce tangible results, we have been commoditized at this level, too. The return on the investment from each of our solutions is likely no different, making the idea of undertaking a change a nonstarter for the client.

The fourth and highest level of value is critical to your success in competitive displacements because it recognizes that a compelling reason to change requires a strategic outcome your competitor is not creating for the client. It shifts the value proposition from the tangible results that your clients perceive as a commodity to the more strategic, future outcomes. The intangibles are what compel change and differentiate you and your solution from your competitors, and you are individually responsible for those intangibles.

The first two parts of this book have been tactical and practical. The frameworks in those sections tell you what you need to do to remove your competitor and replace them. This section of the book will focus on who you have to be to accomplish everything in the earlier chapters. If *you* are the value proposition and *you* have the insight to capture mindshare and *you* are going to be accountable for producing radically better results, then improving the value proposition means improving *your* intangibles.

MINDSHARE AND BEING A 52 PERCENT SME

I have noticed a certain kind of behavior when it comes to subject matter experts (SMEs) and salespeople. As the solutions we sell have grown more technical, we increasingly turn to a subject matter expert to lead parts of a sales conversation. In many sales organizations, the sales force has become so dependent on their SMEs that they cannot imagine making a discovery sales call without having someone with them to address any questions their client might have. There are often twelve legs under the sales force's side of the table when there are only four legs on the client's side. The decision to show up with overwhelming force reeks of fear, but it suggests something even worse.

You cannot be a trusted adviser if you have no advice. Even though your role may be likened to the orchestra conductor, bringing in the right expert at the right time to have the proper conversation, this does not absolve you of the responsibility of being a subject matter expert in your own right.

Your knowledge of the technical components of your solution does not need to match your subject matter expert's, but you also cannot be a know-nothing. You need to have at least 52 percent of your SME's expertise. That means you need to be thoroughly conversant in the first- and second-level questions that any client may ask during a sales call without having a subject matter expert's help. You must be able to demonstrate that you have the knowledge and experience to be able to help your dream client produce a better result—in other words, advice! Let's call this concept the 52 percent SME.

To explain the concept further, if you are the value proposition, you have to be someone who I trust knows as much as or more than I do in a given area. If you know nothing or even less than I do, then I don't need you. You are redundant at best, an annoyance at worst. You are not covering new ground for me, and there are no questions I need you to answer. If I ask you a question and the very best you can do is say, "I know someone who knows that answer," you may be a resource, but you are not a trusted adviser, as you lack the advice. To be a subject matter expert in your own right, you need to have a deep understanding of the trends that should be causing your client to change, the implications of not addressing these trends, and the best choices available when it comes to making a change. You also need to know enough about your solutions that you can tie those solutions to the new outcomes your client needs, as well as explain how those solutions produce the strategic outcomes that would provide your client a better future state—and one worth leaving their current state for.

How do you attain the goal of 52 percent SME? How do you accomplish enough of a knowledge transfer that you can sound like you know almost as much as the SMEs on your team? Achieving this doesn't require that you learn some parlor trick. In fact, all it takes is paying attention.

Every time you call or meet a client with a subject matter expert from your team, write down the questions that the SME asks your prospective client as well as their answers. When your potential client asks the SME a question, write it down and include the SME's response. Unless there is a technical person from the client's side in the room, these questions will be first- and second-level questions, questions that are relatively easy to answer. When you leave the sales call, review the questions and answers with your SME, making sure you understand why they asked those questions, why they gave that particular answer, and why the client asked the questions they did.

If you do the work here, after six or seven sales calls, you will know your SME's shtick. When you can answer the first- and second-level questions, you will no longer need a subject matter expert on initial calls; more important, you will have leveled the playing field with your prospective client.

IRRELEVANCE AVOIDANCE

There are three areas where it is critical that you are a subject matter expert:

Trends That Will Impact Your Client's Business

You must have a deep understanding of the trends that are going to impact your dream client's business. You must be aware of the challenges and opportunities that those trends present. By knowing more than your prospective client, you prevent them from having to do the work to keep up with these things and allow them to outsource that work to you. These trends create the case for change that results in winning new business, but they also provide the foundation for future changes, allowing you to retain your clients by continually developing new initiatives to drive new value. You need to be a subject matter expert on the question "Why should I change now?"

How to Change

It isn't enough to know that your dream client needs to leave your competitor and hire you as their new strategic partner. You also need to know what choices are available to them and how to help them make that change inside their organization. You need to know what is possible. You need to understand how your client can produce the better results that these trends are driving. In an earlier example, I wrote about the significance of one generation retiring in large numbers and companies needing to address this trend by acquiring the people to replace them, as well as building the competencies to train them fast enough to keep pace with this change. This might mean changing their recruiting strategy, modifying the employee value proposition to attract the people they need, building a training curriculum, or some combination of all of these. You need to have a strong opinion about what the right choice is and how to execute the change for and with your client. This is part business acumen, knowing what the correct answer is, and part situational knowledge, understanding how to make trade-offs and decisions around the right solution.

How to Tie Your Solution to Better Results

One of the most important changes you can make is to change the lens through which you view your client's challenges and opportunities. We tend to look at the client, decide they need to change, and pitch them the solution we want to sell (or the one our company compensates us for selling). Instead, you need to view their challenges in terms of the outcomes they need.

Outcomes tie all of these things together. The trends that compel change require that the client get new and better outcomes. The knowledge of how to change is what provides those outcomes. Finally, your solutions help produce those outcomes. The problem with leading with your product is that you get things exactly backward, presenting a solution without first reaching an agreement about what your client needs to do differently.

In order to know the outcome your client needs and tie it to your solution, you have to be a 52 percent SME. You need a strong working knowledge of what product or solution makes the most sense for your client when it comes to driving the new strategic outcomes they need. By starting with the result your prospective client is looking for, you match the product or solution to the outcome, and you address the issue that is creating the need to change.

INTANGIBLES

Most sales leaders and many in the sales improvement business are desperate to believe (and have you believe) that sales is a science. They want to make a complex, dynamic, nonlinear set of human interactions into an engineered, consistent, repeatable process that produces the right result every time. But selling is not science. Selling doesn't even resemble science, even though processes are important.

In science, if I experiment, I get a result. If I repeat that experiment and produce the same effect, I have found some scientific truth. If someone else does the same test under the same conditions and produces the same result, we have scientific proof that our hypothesis is correct. If I do *A*, I will always get *B* as a result. When selling, you can do the same thing that worked in one deal only to have it fail in another.

I am not suggesting that you don't need a sales process and methodologies and frameworks (this is, after all, a book made up of some of these things). But it's important to understand that salespeople can sell the same product for the same company to the same types of clients using the same process and still produce wildly different results. This should make it pretty clear that selling is not a science. The astrophysicist Neil deGrasse Tyson says, "In science, when human behavior enters the equation, things go nonlinear. That's why physics is easy and sociology is hard."

Your dream client needs a compelling reason to remove an existing partner they have worked with for years, and they need to decide that working with you and making you part of their team is better than retaining their existing partner. Alas, you are a huge part of the value proposition.

Likability and Rapport

For a very long time we said of salespeople, "You need to be known, liked, and trusted." And for that same very long time this was true. Now it is only partially true. You also need to create economic and strategic value and have insights and ideas that benefit your client and their business. You have found this idea on every page of this book because it is true, and because it is part of what makes you a trusted adviser.

If you are going to displace your competitor, a large part of that decision will rest on whether the contacts who own this decision have positive feelings about working with you in the future. Those expectations will be shaped by the early meetings where you share your insights and build consensus.

Imagine this scenario. There is one salesperson you like. You can easily see working with them on a daily basis, so much so that you would hire them to be on your team if that were possible. A salesperson from another company is smart, but you wouldn't want to work with them every day. If you have a choice of doing business with someone who is likable and with whom you have rapport, all other things being equal, you choose the person you want to work with, especially if it is over a longer term. Rapport matters because relationships matter.

There is one other area of likability that we need to touch on here. There is a major difference between being likable and "needing to be liked." Having a pleasant personality is one thing, being a people pleaser is another—and detrimental to your success. Needing to be liked makes people avoid difficult conversations and conflict at all costs. Being likable means you possess the ability to connect with people, to listen to and understand their needs, to care about them and make them feel important, and to be pleasant to be around. All of these things make it easier to discuss the difficult issues where conflict is present.

Being likable is a competitive advantage. Needing to be liked is an enormous disadvantage.

Business Acumen

We've spent a fair bit of time on this throughout the book and especially in this chapter. You now know that creating and winning new opportunities is in large part a measure of your business acumen. You also know that you build the foundation of your relationships with your clients on your ability to serve them as a trusted adviser, strategic partner, and good counsel.

Let's go back to our two salespeople, the one you like and the one you don't like nearly as well. What if the one you like is a know-nothing? What if the one you aren't crazy about is a stone-cold subject matter expert? Now you are conflicted, wanting to work with someone who is a good cultural fit but needing someone who can really help.

Let's add a third salesperson to this scenario. You like the third salesperson, and they are wicked smart. This person has just resolved your conflict, haven't they? Likable and smart are not mutually exclusive, and do not believe anyone who tells you they are. You have to be this third salesperson.

Caring

A potential publisher of my first book, *The Only Sales Guide You'll Ever Need* (a rather unfortunate title for a book by a person who continues to publish more books on sales), hated the chapter I wrote on caring. He was confused as to why the concept showed up in a book on sales. What he didn't understand is that sales stopped being a self-oriented endeavor for most of us a long time ago (even if the stereotype persists). It is more than ever an other-oriented effort; we are serving others.

I want you to think about preference here. Your dream client has a choice of working with a self-oriented person who projects that they care about getting ink on paper more than the better results they need or an other-oriented person who is bent on helping them drive better results and will be accountable for doing so. If your dream client has to work with you and your company for years after hiring you, the decision they are making is around who they want on their team.

Why would they choose to work with someone who treats them like a transaction? Like every intangible in this chapter, possessing the attribute of caring makes it easy to prefer to work with you, especially over a complacent provider who long ago gave up caring and believes they have an absolute right to their client's business.

Attitude

It's unlikely that anyone would prefer to work with someone who is pessimistic, cynical, skeptical, and unengaged over someone who is the opposite in every way. When you are courting your dream client, they are deciding whether or not they want you on their team. Why on earth would they choose someone who has a negative attitude or lousy energy?

Who you are matters as much as or more than what you sell. You demonstrate who you are by how you sell. It's a large part of what makes up preference, the single factor from the earlier chapters that helps you gain a decision to move from your competitor to you. Having a positive, optimistic, future-oriented, can-do, will-do, "I own it" attitude helps to create a preference to work with you.

It's important to note here that if you are so unengaged with your work that you have no passion for what you are doing, your prospective client will recognize it, realizing that this is the person they will be adding to their team. Your dream client already has enough unengaged people who are biding their time, going through the motions, and punching a clock.

At the time I am writing this, many others who write about sales are applauding the idea that you no longer need to be the gregarious, outgoing, smile-on-your-face, shine-on-your-shoes salesperson of the past. Let's correct this mistake here and get to what is right. The truth is that if those attributes are phony and being employed as tactics, they are to be avoided. But know for sure that you do need to have an upbeat, engaged, and enthu-siastic energy. You need to have a positive attitude that is seen and felt to create a preference for you.

One last word here. Your attitude has to be seen and felt in every client interaction. You can have a day off, but you cannot have an off day.

Presence

I once had a prospective client say to me, "I can't believe you drove all the way out here to see me. You didn't need to do that." In fact, that is why I did it; I knew no one else would drive that far for a meeting. As you might expect, we ended up doing business together.

We live in an age when technology is a dominant factor. All of us, without ever making the conscious decision to do so, now live behind three screens. We are almost never without a computer in front of us. If we are away from that screen, we have the tablet close at hand. And we are never, ever more than thirty-six inches away from our smartphones.

Technology has changed the media we use to communicate. Now, again without any real conscious decision, email is the dominant medium of business conversations. Using email for sales conversations is to exchange effectiveness for efficiency—a trade-off you should never make.

If you are trying to create a preference to work with you instead of your competitor, having a presence will tip things in your direction. The person who shows up is the person who is committed to the client and their business. The person who takes the time to see the client's facility, to meet the stakeholders and develop relationships, and to understand their business and their needs is the person who is stacking the deck in their favor. Showing up is an indication that you care, that your prospective client is important to you. I can't imagine even trying to displace a competitor without gaining access to the building and the people inside it. You should never try to replace your competitor without a presence. You will make things more difficult than they have to be.

Someone once said that a large part of success is merely showing up. Those words have never been truer than they are today.

Your Process

The process with which you engage your client can be an advantage. I recently received an email from a salesperson who was struggling to win clients. He explained his process in an email, noting that it consisted of asking the client for the opportunity to give them a quote for his services. His request was continually rejected. This approach is an extreme example of a salesperson in B2B sales transacting as if it were a B2C sale. The process here does not in any way create value for the client. It is eliminating a chance to build an opportunity and a preference.

Think about the opportunities you have to create a preference to work with you and your company and to have the client believe that your solution is the one that will serve them best. The first opportunities are sales interactions with the client. What do you do with those interactions? Do you help them understand why they should change, how they should do something different, what their choices are, and how they might produce breakthrough results? Do you serve them by knowing how to help them with a process, ensuring that they know what commitments they need to make and how those commitments serve them? Are you consultative, or are you sometimes something less than that?

You can think about your company's sales process here, but I want you to think about what you do. The decision to buy from you instead of retaining your competitor boils down to whether or not your dream client believes you are a better partner to move forward with into the future. You need to engage with them in a way that increases their preference to work with you. Your understanding as to what needs to happen to produce a better future state and the steps required to get there is an intangible that tilts the playing field in your direction.

I have written about these next three attributes in a prior book. I have woven them into dozens of blog posts at www.thesalesblog.com over the years, believing that these mind-set attributes are critical components of success.

Ability to Lead

Leadership is not something that sales organizations train their salespeople in. We don't think about salespeople as leaders, but that doesn't mean the client doesn't recognize and value a salesperson's ability to lead. If we had to roll up all the reasons that your dream clients may be dissatisfied with their current partners, you could put them all under one label: "a failure of leadership." That failure paves the way for a competitive displacement.

Why? Leadership is taking accountability for producing a result. Even though you will find countless books and blog posts and LinkedIn entries that describe the long list of attributes that make one a great leader, like vision, people skills, and character, all these attributes are in the service of one thing: being accountable for producing a better future state. As a salesperson, your responsibility is no different. The willingness to lead, to be accountable for producing better results, gives you a massive advantage in a competitive displacement. If your dream client's existing partner has not been willing or able to lead their team and the client's team in producing better results, your leadership creates a preference to work with you. Odds are, your competitor doesn't demonstrate leadership.

One of the primary questions your dream client is considering when they choose you to displace their current partner is whether they believe you will produce the better result you promise. They want to know that you are going to move heaven and earth to produce that result, working with them to influence their team to make changes, and working with your team to ensure that they execute. They want a partner, not someone who will disappear once they sign on the dotted line and leave it to someone else to deal with the challenges that may arise.

As my friend Mark Hunter says, "Sales is leadership, and leadership is sales." Leadership, and looking like a leader, is a strong intangible.

Resourcefulness

I was once speaking to a group of former Special Forces soldiers. One of them used an acronym with which I was unfamiliar. As they talked about a tough problem, one gentleman said to the other, "FITFO." I asked, "What is FITFO?" The ex–spec op soldier repeated, "FITFO." Not understanding, I asked again, "What is FITFO?" only to receive the same reply and a smile. The soldier then said, "Figure it the f*** out!"

I discovered that this is one of the standard operating procedures for special operators and soldiers. They get dropped off to complete some mission, and they are expected to run into unanticipated challenges for which they will have difficulty getting support and where there is no easy answer. So they have to figure out what to do in the most difficult of circumstances. It's a good operating principle for salespeople, too.

If your dream client knew how to produce the better result they needed, they'd already be producing that result. If they knew how to have the internal conversations and build consensus around that initiative, they'd already have done so. Moreover, if your competitor knew how to help them do better and cared enough to force the issue, your dream client would not need you. But none of these things are true, and this is why you have to be resourceful enough to figure out how to help them produce better results.

A good part of competitive displacement is built on solving problems that have long gone unresolved. Creating an opportunity and winning that opportunity come from being resourceful enough to figure out how to help the client with the process of changing, especially when there are obstacles and opponents who are slavishly devoted to protecting their silo and the status quo. In this way, selling shares a certain similarity with the Special Forces soldiers. Your sales process doesn't speak to many of the challenges you face when creating an opportunity to displace your competitor or the challenges you face once you've won.

One thing I can promise you with high confidence is that your prospective client is looking for someone with the resourcefulness to figure out how to help them improve their results. But not just resourcefulness, as that indicates doing something once a problem reveals itself. Your resourcefulness needs to come with a good bit of initiative. How do you give your prospective client the experience that proves you are going to be proactive? How do you help them recognize that you will not be a reactive, passive partner who will wait until something goes wrong before you act (something they are likely already experiencing and a source of their challenges and frustration now)? Throughout the process of working to displace your competitor, you have to prove that you are proactive, that you are buttoned up, detail oriented, and working to be in front of any challenges.

Thoughtfulness

Thoughtfulness is really a part of caring and being other oriented. It isn't given anywhere near the attention it deserves. In life, it is the little things that are really the big things. It is sometimes the smallest of gestures that make the largest of impacts.

A handwritten card is something different from an email thanking the client for their time and their help. A text message to ask your dream client for their coffee order on your way to meet with them is caring in action, exceeded by remembering their request and not asking before your next meeting. The call to follow up consistently made. The small commitments consistently kept.

A Sense of Humor

If there is an intangible that overindexes on producing a preference, it is a sense of humor. I'll generalize this attribute even more and suggest it is the ability to entertain. Your dream client has to live with you after they hire you, and you need to be someone with whom they want to work. That said, why would they want to work with a humorless bore?

There will always be issues that arise when you are pursuing and serving your dream clients. The person who can inject a little levity into those situations without appearing to minimize the challenge has a significant advantage when it comes to creating a preference. The levity can remove some of the stress, and it can demonstrate your optimism and the confidence that together you will resolve the issue, that you will FITFO.

One of my favorite books is *The Little Prince,* written by a French air force pilot named Antoine de Saint-Exupéry. My favorite quote from that book nicely sums up this entire chapter and the case for developing the intangibles: "What is essential is invisible to the eye."

DO THIS NOW

1. Write down three or four things you need to learn to be a 52 percent subject matter expert in the intersection between your industry and your clients.

2. Make a list of attributes in which you are deficient now and would like to improve. For help with this, go to www.theonlysalesguide .com and pick up that book.

   To download the worksheet that accompanies this chapter, go to www.eattheirlunch.training.

Chapter 10

BECOMING A TRUSTED ADVISER AND CONSULTATIVE SALESPERSON

IF YOU LISTEN TO SALESPEOPLE TALK ABOUT HOW THEY WANT to sell, without fail you'll hear the words "consultative" and "trusted adviser." If you press them to describe what makes one's approach consultative, many who use this word will have a tough time describing what exactly would make them consultative. In most cases, what the person means by "consultative" is that they don't want to be anything that hearkens back to the days of aggressive, high-pressure, manipulative sales practices. In that their definition would be correct but incomplete.

It isn't enough that you are a nonpushy type of salesperson. That by itself is not enough to make you consultative, and it may even indicate to the client that you are conflict averse, preferring to avoid difficult conversations and possessing a strong need for your client to like you. Being truly consultative means being a trusted adviser, and that is a much higher bar than most imagine. Knowing how to tie your solution to your client's needs does not get you over that bar. The "adviser" part isn't so simple, and it requires more business acumen and situational knowledge than most salespeople possess. It requires an information disparity, with you having more knowledge than your client as it pertains to the area where you provide advice. When you suggest that your client "knows more about their business than I do," that is clear proof that you are not a trusted adviser. What could you be advising them on if they know more than you? You have to know more about where your industry and their business intersect.

In this chapter, we'll work on tilting the playing field in your direction and helping you develop into a trusted adviser and consultative salesperson in a way that will be both seen and felt.

HOW TO GAIN THE ABILITY TO ADVISE

Way back in chapter 2 you were required to identify the four or five trends that would impact your dream client's business over the next eighteen to twenty-four months as a way to begin the process of helping them discover a reason to change and start the process of displacing your competitor. When you tie your client's future challenges and your best ideas and solutions to those challenges together, you are acting as a trusted adviser. By providing the insights that help your prospective clients avoid risks, capitalize on opportunities, and produce a better future outcome through the actions you recommend, you are shaping that future.

Know the Strategic Outcomes You Create

You now know that there are four levels of value that you create, with Level 3 being tangible outcomes. Those tangible outcomes might easily be expressed as increased revenue, increased profit, and decreased costs, as these are the big drivers of value. But strategic outcomes are different, and they may not all be easy to measure. For instance, increased market share is a strategic outcome, and as you move up to senior levels, this outcome may be far more important than cost savings. Market share can be measured, even if it isn't as easy to capture as cost savings.

There are other strategic outcomes senior leaders pursue that are outside of direct and tangible measures such as revenue, profit, and costs. They may have a strategic imperative to retain their clients, develop new offerings, increase their speed to market, open new markets, bring new products to market, or develop new strategies or capabilities. Right now, many leaders are trying to determine how to create a digital business before they lose market share to more agile competitors.

You may or may not know what a company's leadership team is focused on, but you must be adept at tying your solution to something strategic. If they want to "retain their clients" as a strategic initiative, you have to be able to say, "The trends that we shared with you about technology in your space point to the idea that if your business doesn't allow your customers to order and communicate on the web, you will lag your competitors and lose customers by not meeting this expectation."

The reason strategic outcomes are worth more than tangible outcomes alone is that they are more systemic, more important, and they demand that something be done. They compel change, whereas a marginal improvement at Level 3 may not. Being strategic and initiating improvements helps to move you from salesperson to trusted adviser.

Serving Your Client and Controlling the Process

How many times is your dream client going to decide to buy what you sell over the course of their career? For some purchases, that number will be as low as two or three times at most. For other investments, the buyer may buy half a dozen times. How many times will you sell your product or solution over the course of your career in sales? Hundreds? Maybe thousands?

You cannot be consultative and a trusted adviser if you are not willing to deal with conflict over the process of serving your prospective client. We have to spend some time here talking about conflict and collaboration and the intersection of the two. Conflict is part of business and part of sales because it is part of human behavior. It comes with the territory. In sales, conflict shows up all over the place; some disputes are small and not very meaningful, while others are much larger, more charged, and more difficult, all of which you need to manage. If conflict is present, collaboration is possible.

The first place you run into conflict is asking your dream client for their time and exploring change. If they have a partner they have used for years that they also very much enjoy working with, your request presents a threat to that relationship. If you show up talking about how things need to change, the very idea of going through the process of doing something different can create internal conflict, especially if it means what your dream client is doing now is somehow wrong. It can be perceived as an attack, even if there is nothing in your delivery that would suggest that you are critical. As conflicts go, these are relatively weak and quickly resolved. One of the ways you can prevent your dream client from feeling that your exploration of new possibilities is a threat to what they are doing now or compels them to defend their existing partner is to offer the conversation as an exploration. By suggesting that you are simply exploring ideas, you reduce their need to defend. You might also suggest that your contact will have a good deal of knowledge about the ideas you explore, preventing them from feeling any threat to their ego or feeling that you are being disrespectful (which, by the way, makes you more likable and generates greater rapport).

As you start to develop a solution, there can be internal conflicts over what the right solution is. When you are helping your client build consensus, the obstacles and opponents in chapters 7 and 8 can create political conflicts. People may start to defend their silo, the source of their power. I have personally both won and lost deals due to political conflicts that either forced a decision to retain a current provider or forced a move to my company. In one of these situations, my dream client said, "Hiring you would be political suicide. There is no doubt that you are the better choice, but I would lose my job to go against my boss on this one." Naturally, I lost that round, although they did find another place where we could do business.

There is almost invariably conflict about pricing and terms because we as salespeople have allowed our clients to underinvest in the results they need for decades, promising them that they can have better, faster, and cheaper. Is it a surprise that they now believe that better, faster, cheaper is what they should be looking for in a value proposition? The commitment to make an adequate investment creates conflict. In a litigious society like ours, you are going to have disputes over terms, especially around indemnification and risks. The reason I describe these conflicts as being part of the need to control the process is that the contacts within your dream client company will try to avoid conflicts, and in doing so, create greater conflicts.

Without the commitment to collaborate on a solution, the client creates a more significant conflict when the solution doesn't serve some population of their business. By deciding that it would be easier for you to give them your best ideas without considering what might need to be configured or customized for some group specifically, they open up the risk of buying the solution and then discovering that it doesn't work for that area of the business. Or they sit down with their peers to discuss your proposal only to find out that their peers are opposed, killing the initiative and leaving its dead carcass on the boardroom table in the form of a proposal and PowerPoint deck. Without having their needs considered, the stakeholders who oppose your initiative are right to do so.

The commitment to match the investment to the outcome also creates conflict. Once purchasing or supply chain or some economic buyer enters the scene, you have likely found a stakeholder who believes that "value always equals lower price and a good supplier can help us produce better results and also reduce the investment we are making in those results." I recently listened to what I believed to be an enlightened supply chain manager tell a group of "suppliers" that he needed them to invest more in the relationship and to save his company money without lowering their prices. Later he sent a note telling the bidders to lower their prices. I have yet to find any scenario where investing less produces a better result, but I have countless examples where pulling money out of a solution produces poorer results—even if the real damage isn't seen until much later. Alas, there is always a conflict over the difference between price and cost, the price being more easily quantified, and costs being seen as entirely subjective.

When you struggle with your dream client over bringing other stakeholders into the process to gain their support, that decision most likely leads to your losing an opportunity. Because they want to avoid the conflict of dealing with obstacles, opponents, and the process of building consensus, your prospective client opens themselves up to coping with more conflict and challenges in the future by waiting too long to change.

These are some of the conflicts that come from the decision as to who controls the process. They crop up because your dream client doesn't want to deal with the conflicts that arise with change, and the decision to avoid those conflicts causes a different set of struggles, most of which will destroy the initiative to change. As a trusted adviser, you must work to control the process, engaging in these conflicts and helping the contacts within your client's company navigate them.

Can you imagine a trusted adviser who says nothing as the person they advise makes one wrong decision after another because they want to avoid having difficult conversations? Can you picture a trusted adviser who so desperately wants their prospective client's business that they are willing to say nothing about the mistakes their client is making in order to avoid offending their client? One who is consultative and aspires to be a trusted adviser must speak truth to power, come what may. There is every reason to challenge without being challenging.

A Collaborative Approach

A consultative sale requires a collaborative approach. You are working on problems, challenges, and opportunities with your prospective client. They are part of the process, and they need to participate in the change initiative.

The antidote to conflict is collaboration. It is also part of what makes you consultative. We've said that the role of trusted adviser requires trust and advice. Collaboration creates greater trust and improves your ability to help your dream client take action on your advice. You might think of this as your bedside manner, how you approach things, especially conflict.

Collaboration means exercising your resourcefulness together with your dream client to identify choices and make decisions. The challenge for most of us is that we too quickly get wrapped around the axle, believing that we know the right answer. Because we have seen a certain client challenge before, we think we can apply our prior experience to any similar problem or challenge, neglecting to analyze all four quadrants we looked at in chapter 5. We humans are great at generalizing, which is necessary and useful. You don't need to reassess how a doorknob works every time you encounter a new door; it's pretty certain to work like other doorknobs. But it's important to remember that selling is not something you are doing to someone. It is something you are doing for someone and with someone. The "with someone" is the part we are concerned about here, especially as it pertains to being consultative. Even though you may know what has worked for other clients in the past, the contacts you are working with may know more about what will work for them, how your idea may need to be modified, and what they can actually execute now. It's equally important that your prospective client contributes to the solution, that they have a chance to share ideas, and that they discover what they believe is necessary to move forward. You deprive them of this when you run right past this part of the process. Collaboration strengthens your chances of sitting down to a fine meal made up exclusively of your competitor's lunch.

A consultative approach is one in which you are comfortable making suggestions even as you invite your dream clients to share their thoughts, their ideas, their preferences, and how they believe things should be done. The positive outcomes from this approach are many. First, by your inviting your dream client into the process with you, they become invested. They have ownership of the process, the outcomes, and the solution, increasing their commitment to pursue and defend the change you are helping them make. If this were all that you gained from a collaborative approach, it would be enough to make it a worthwhile strategy. Second, and equally important, the process of collaboration increases engagement and reduces resistance. There is a reason that the word "salesperson" carries so much baggage. It's because so many salespeople used high-pressure tactics and were so self-oriented for so long that the negative connotation stuck. By collaborating on what comes next and how you get there, you're eliminating the possibility that your dream client feels like they've lost all control. By working with your client, you reduce any need for resistance on your dream client's part because they are involved in the decisions you make together going forward.

Finally, as much as experience tells us that we know the right answer to what our dream clients need to do to produce better results, we don't often know enough about the specifics of their business (even when we have a serious grasp of their industry). There are some areas where your client will know way more than you, like their processes and the complicated map of stakeholders who will be affected by a decision to change. We may also be unaware of the challenges our proposals might create for them. You can be completely right about the solution and utterly wrong about what it will take to implement and execute that solution in any particular company. Collaboration closes this knowledge gap.

Collaboration provides the conversations that help you find a path forward. You say, "I think we need to deal with the IT director because he is opposed to what we are doing here, and we need to hear his objections and concerns. How do we do that without making things worse, and in some way that we might gain his support? Or at least allow him to stand down?" Collaborating is one of the most powerful ways you move through conflict, and it is part of a consultative approach.

Impartiality

I once had a dream client who needed help. I had pursued the dream client for a long enough time that I was excited by the first opportunity to work with them. As we discussed the company's needs, it was immediately clear that mine wasn't the right company to handle them. I offered to refer the contact to someone who was better suited to handle his company's needs. My refusal to take his business had the effect of making him push harder for me to partner with his company. Because we weren't the right choice for them, we declined.

If you want to be consultative, you have to be impartial. We need to work carefully through this because it can be a little confusing. You will be pulled in two different directions. Because you are in sales, you have to believe genuinely in your company and what you do. You have to believe that you are better than your competitors. You are a strong advocate for your company. At the same time, you have to believe that it is your job to provide your dream client with the best advice possible, even if it means recommending they do nothing, referring them to someone else, or refusing their business. Let's look at two scenarios to make the distinction between believing in your company and being impartial.

Scenario number one: You happen to stumble across your dream client at the moment they have a rather serious need for help. Your dream client needs a reduction in the price of what you sell because they are losing money and their client will not allow them to pass off a price increase. In this case, your competitor with a lower price will actually increase their costs because their product is inferior, inadequate, and fails at a rate that is three times higher than your solution's. Your solution has a higher price, but will lower their costs by eliminating the amount of rework the company needs to do. By reducing their losses in the process, you can help them turn a profit on this account. In this case, your higher price is more than offset by the expense of your dream client's rework. In this scenario, your higher price benefits the client, and it is your responsibility to make the dream client understand that a lower price will not benefit them in the long run.

Now let's look at scenario number two: You encounter a similar scenario to the one I just described. Your dream client needs a price reduction on something you sell because they are losing money and their biggest customer will not tolerate a price increase. Even though your solution will last longer than your competitor's lower-priced solution, your very best price will not help them lower their price. In this case, the durability of what you sell will reduce costs, but those cost savings would be passed down to your dream client's customer, and there is no willingness on the customer's part to pay more. Here, unfortunately, there is no scenario in which your dream client can acquire the outcome they need by buying your higher-priced solution. By selling something better even at the same price, your dream client is put in no better position than they were when you found them. In this case, your dream client needs something you can't give them, a lower price. There is no offset from the rework in this case. Selling them something with a higher price does not in any way benefit them, even if it benefits their customer.

Let's now look at a new scenario that is more difficult and more interesting. Let's say you sell a service, and your competitor sells a similar service at a lower price. Your service, however, is higher touch, higher value, and higher caring. You are easier to do business with, and you deliver a better experience. Besides the fact that the experience is better (Level 2), the outcomes (Level 3) are precisely the same. You are not being impartial by suggesting that your lower-priced competitor is a better choice. In this case, there is differentiation. Your price is higher because you are creating greater value.

I am making this point for a fundamental reason. Too many salespeople who compete in competitive markets, red oceans, if you will, believe that their company is not competitive because they have higher prices than their competitors. They believe "good enough" is good enough and that their "best-in-class" solution that creates greater value is not worth paying more to obtain. Believing that a lower price is an indication of greater value is a fundamental error, and it is not impartiality. Instead, it's an admission that the salesperson is having a tough time differentiating their offering and believes that selling should be easier.

If what you are attempting to sell your dream client will not ultimately benefit them, don't sell it to them. If something else will produce the result they need, but acquiring it means buying something else from someone else, recommend that they do so and retain your role as trusted adviser. If what you sell is more challenging to sell because you can create greater value, but at a higher price point, be completely partial to your solution and work hard to differentiate the value you create. Do everything in your power to sell that solution to your dream client.

Justifying the Delta

You must be able to help your prospective clients invest more to produce better results. One of the biggest mistakes salespeople and sales organizations make is allowing their clients to underinvest in the results they need. A big, big part of this is the inability of the salesperson to justify the delta between what the client is currently investing and what they need to spend. Doing so requires some work and a lot of confidence.

If your dream client isn't getting the result they need, one of the causes may be that they are not investing enough to produce that result. In every business, there are soft costs, those costs that are difficult to capture and quantify. Everyone knows about them and believes they exist, but they also know that reducing the soft costs may require an additional investment of money, time, and energy.

I spent much of my life in the staffing business, so I will use that as an example here. The price of a markup on a contingent or contract employee might be 50 percent above the employee's pay rate. I once shared our pricing with a vice president of human resources for a global company with which we were working. As we reviewed our results (which were outstanding), he said, "Your prices are outrageous! How do you justify this?!" I replied, "We're advertising, recruiting, conducting background checks, paying benefits, paying matching taxes, paying for worker's compensation, and eking out a net margin of about four percent. What is your internal burden on a full-time employee?" The VP of human resources looked at me and said, "Our internal burden is just over seventy-four percent fully loaded. I should have known that you have all the same costs we do. I get it." Our price was 24 percent lower than the cost to him of a fully loaded employee, an employee with full benefits. And that was the end of our conversation about our price. I justified the delta by helping him recognize his real costs and how much he was saving.

Turnover is expensive. It requires that people be rehired, retrained, and onboarded into a new role. It also means a loss of productivity when the employee leaves and the job is unfilled, as well as a loss of productivity while a new employee is getting up to speed. In some roles, like sales, a vacant position equals an opportunity cost that is measured in millions of dollars in revenue and profit.

- What does it cost your client not to have the product when they need it?
- What does it cost them to have the product fail?
- What does it cost to replace the product, and what are the costs associated with that failure?
- What does it cost the client to have to do rework or accept returns from failed products?
- What does it cost them to acquire the product?
- What is the opportunity cost?

• What are the challenges and problems that require workarounds costing the client?

It is your job to justify the delta between the investment your dream client is currently making and the investment they need to make. Being consultative means thinking broadly here, including the financial investment, the investment of time, and the investment of energy. In the case of one client who felt that we were too expensive, we asked them if they could invest more time and energy in taking care of their people—without spending any more money than they were spending with us. We produced a better outcome with an investment that, at the time, was mistakenly perceived as being more expensive than it would be to handle everything we did themselves.

Creating Value

Value creation requires relational value, the ability to be known, liked, and trusted. And it requires strategic and economic value. You have to produce real results.

This section will be intentionally short. One of the most important factors in being consultative is the creation of value for your dream clients. The value that you create is found not only in the product, the experience of using your solution, the outcomes your solution generates, or even the strategic results you produce for the client. Value is also a measurement of who you are and how you sell.

This makes your knowledge about what needs to be done and why a key variable. Your expertise as to how to produce new and better results is also a measurement of value, just as knowing what to do but not understanding how to help the particular dream client you are working with make the necessary changes in their company is not value. Knowing what needs to be done and lacking the ability to sell that change may be exactly the position your competitor is in right now, knowing what needs to change but being unable to help the client initiate and make that change. Your knowledge of the trade-offs that your prospective client might need to make to produce better results helps them make better decisions, and that is value. In the red ocean, it pays to be the great white shark. The great white rules the red ocean. To be consultative and a trusted adviser, you need to create more value than anyone else by being super consultative, being collaborative while controlling the process, being impartial, and justifying the delta between your solution and the existing partner's. All of these differentiating skills and attributes help build executive presence, the subject of the next chapter and an intangible that allows your dream client to perceive an extreme difference between you and their existing partner.

DO THIS NOW

1. What are three strategic outcomes you help your clients create?

2. What commitments does the client have to agree to for you to control the process in a way that ensures that they get the better outcomes they need? For more on controlling the process, go to www .thelostartofclosing.com for a guide to understanding and gaining the ten commitments.

To download the worksheet that accompanies this chapter, go to www.eattheirlunch.training.

Chapter 11

DEVELOPING AN
EXECUTIVE PRESENCE

IF YOU WANT TO TAKE BUSINESS FROM YOUR COMPETITOR, you have to be someone your dream client is willing to displace their current provider—and likely their friend—to obtain. Executive presence is the ability to present yourself as someone with the knowledge, skills, and capability to help lead your dream client's company forward. Executive presence differentiates you, making you someone others would want on their team—and someone they hope is not on their competitor's team. The first thing you need to build an executive presence is confidence. You need to look and sound like you belong in the room with the leadership team of your dream client, and they have to recognize you as a peer, as someone with domain authority. How you carry yourself matters a great deal. The question we need to answer here is, "How do you develop that executive presence, that level of confidence?" Let's break this down into component parts that you can develop—and have been developing throughout this book.

DEVELOP AN INFORMED OPINION
AND A POINT OF VIEW

A trusted adviser's advice comes from having a strong, informed opinion and a point of view as to why and how your dream client should change. You have to know what external (and sometimes, internal) factors are going to disrupt your dream client's business in the future, or the root causes of why they are struggling now. Your insight has to provide you with some point of view about what's going on that is affecting their business. You must be able to share your view with your dream client.

I've heard salespeople say things like "They're running a business. They know all the things that are going on that will impact their business. They don't need me to tell them these things." This is woefully incorrect. It is more likely that your client doesn't know everything that you know when you do the work in chapter 2 to capture mindshare. Your dream client spends their time trying to work on their own business, and they are mostly head down dealing with the daily problems and challenges of their business. Moreover, you have a point of view about the implications of the trends and factors that are affecting their business, as well as what they should do in response.

Having a point of view is more than knowing what's going on; it is also having strong opinions about what should be done. I know that some people who read these words or hear me speak them chafe at the idea that they should have a point of view and strong opinions. But unless you have ideas you can argue for and strongly recommend to your dream client, why should they bother with you at all? This is not to suggest that you will not invite disagreement and the opportunity for your dream client to help shape your thinking. The fact that you have a point of view can create a constructive tension that allows for both you and your dream client to discover something that creates new possibilities. It's also important to note that there is no reason to be so entrenched and argumentative that you cause your dream client to decide you are too pigheaded to be someone they want on their team.

You picked up this book because you wanted to learn how to displace your competitors and eat their lunch. You'd be disappointed if you opened the book to find that its author didn't have very strong ideas about how to do that, didn't challenge you to create greater value, didn't require you to capture mindshare, prospect with purpose, understand the stakeholders you need to remove and replace your competitor, and build consensus. I don't pretend to be neutral: I have a clear point of view and a set of opinions that are expressed throughout this book. You need informed opinions and a point of view that you are willing to defend if you want to have an executive presence.

When you have a point of view and an informed opinion favoring some course of action, you are going to get pushback. Not to worry. We'll handle that later in this chapter.

AVOID INFORMATION PARITY

Sustaining relationships requires that you continually learn more so that you can bring new insights and ideas.

There is another part of executive presence that is very closely tied to your bias and point of view. That component is information disparity. If you and your client both have the exact same knowledge, you are redundant. If they know everything you know, then they don't need you to advise them. You have to create an imbalance in information.

It's useful to think of it this way: You are your dream client's second brain. While they are busy working in their business, you are doing the heavy lifting of reading and listening and studying what is going on in the world that may impact their business. You are continually searching for new insights and new ideas to bring to their business to keep them ahead of their competitors. The work that you do to be a trusted adviser allows your dream client to outsource their thinking about the things that fall into the intersection of their business and your business, so they don't have to do it. When you have an asymmetry of information in your favor, you have a useful component of executive presence.

As John Adams, one of the founders of the United States, said, "Facts are stubborn things; and whatever may be our wishes, our inclinations, or the dictates of our passions, they cannot alter the state of facts and evidence." Facts truly are stubborn things. In a meeting with an executive, an excellent command of the facts creates information disparity. This is why earlier in this book, I noted that eleven thousand baby boomers are retiring every day in America. The fact that such a large generation is retiring in such high numbers is a trend that will impact many businesses. What that impact may be can vary from industry to industry, in some cases bringing challenges, like hiring people to fill the jobs that boomers are leaving, and for others it creates opportunities, like greater demand for insurance plans.

At the time of this writing, driverless trucks are being built and tested. At some point, these trucks will be safer than actual drivers. When the price and safety reach the level where drivers are no longer necessary, around 3.5 million over-the-road drivers will have to find a new profession. We can argue about whether this is a good thing or a bad thing. We can argue about the timeline. We can even argue about the morality of displacing humans with robots. We cannot, however, argue about the fact that there are 3.5 million drivers at risk of being put out of a job in the coming decades.

The takeaway here is that you have to know things if you want to have an executive presence. You have to have facts that allow you to make your case and defend your point of view. You must have proof that what you say is true and that supports your position that change is necessary, as well as what that change needs to include.

When you say something like "The client knows their business better than I do," you are correct in the micro sense (their company) and incorrect in the macro sense (you should know more than they do about their industry and how your business intersects with theirs). This is an information imbalance, having more information than the prospective client does as it pertains to your business at the intersection with your dream client's business.

DON'T BE CONFLICT AVERSE

In the previous chapter, we discussed how to handle conflict over the process, but I want to bring you back to conflict here as it pertains to having an executive presence. Most of the executives you encounter are likely to be extraordinarily comfortable with conflict. It is in part how they ended up in their position. This can sometimes make them difficult characters.

That said, some of the conflict they create is tactical. They push back on your bias and point of view or your interpretation of the facts to see if you really have the chops and are really committed to your ideas. They create conflict to test whether you are going to stand up to their challenge and defend your case.

At one point in his long tenure with General Electric, the legendary CEO Jack Welch was buying and selling a company almost every day. His leadership team was bringing him new opportunities at a blistering clip. When someone would show up to present, Welch would tear into their idea. He'd tell them the idea was terrible and ask them why they would even consider it. He'd forcefully insist that it didn't make sense for the business. If the person bringing the idea backed down, he wouldn't take action on it. If they gave a full-throated defense of the opportunity, he'd consider it.

It wasn't the idea that Welch was testing. He was testing to see if the person making the recommendation believed in it deeply enough to defend it, and whether they would be willing to execute if he gave them the green light.

I'd like to tell you that conflict is rare in sales, that you won't run into it often enough for it to be a concern. But when you are helping your dream client decide to change, there will be conflict. When you are asking them to fire their friends, there will be conflict. As you are working with stakeholders who are obstacles or opponents of the change you are recommending, there will be conflict. Not all of that conflict will be a test of how much you believe what you are saying and whether or not you can be trusted to deliver the outcomes you sell.

Being comfortable in conflict can be made easier if you can approach it from a point of view that reduces your emotional response to it. One way to view someone who is creating conflict is to understand why they are doing what they're doing. In almost every case, you will find their fears.

The task of removing your competitor will fall to someone, maybe the stakeholder who has had a long relationship with the people they work with there. The people who will need to change what they are doing now and who are already overwhelmed are creating conflict and pushing back because they fear what the change will require of them. Some executive will be afraid the change you are making is going to move power from them to someone else in the organization, and they may go to great lengths to protect their power.

The view you take of this should be clinical if you want to develop the capacity to be comfortable with conflict. You are observing the person's emotional state or challenge, and even though you are the catalyst for change, you are there to help the company and the people who work there produce better results. You should be clinical, objective, and maintain a level of emotional distance from any conflict that arises, even if you are being personally attacked. Never get sucked into responding with personal attacks or finger pointing. Keep your goal in mind and keep your cool at all times.

BE A COMBATIVE DIPLOMAT

One of the attributes that gives one an executive presence is the ability to challenge the status quo, challenge ideas, and challenge perspectives without being a challenging person. This is a difference worth noting.

When you are engaged in the process of helping people change and produce better results, the process generally comes with a good deal of conflict. Asking people to stop doing what they've always done, what they've been rewarded for doing, and what they're comfortable with isn't easy. You must be willing and able to challenge the status quo—and to do so in a way that allows people to agree to change. There is no benefit from being a challenging personality where there is already inherent conflict.

"What you are doing is wrong, outdated, and costing you money. You need to do it differently." As soon as you say the word "wrong," you have created resistance in the person or people to whom you are speaking. You have now made them feel the need to defend who they are and what they are doing. In short, you have created resistance to change by being a challenging personality. Diplomacy is what is called for here.

"It looks like you are working really hard here. You may have already seen something like the idea we want to share with you. This idea might make it easier and faster for you to get the same or better results than you're getting now. Can I share a couple things we see people doing that help them eliminate some of the challenges you might be dealing with now?" What comes after this is the new idea, which means change, and the change itself is the challenge. The new way of viewing their business and a new approach is the challenge. You do not benefit from being the challenge, or the target of those who oppose change.

To challenge people to see their business through a new and different lens, to challenge them to make real change, to challenge them to remove your competitor, you want to eliminate resistance—not create it. You want to collaborate wherever there is conflict. You want to win support, not create opposition.

TALK ABOUT FAILURE

Being a trusted adviser means you have to deal with the most difficult, most strategic issues and opportunities. You have to help tackle the big stuff.

During a recent sales kickoff meeting, I watched two executives speak to the company's sales force about what they needed to do to be a good strategic partner. Both executives, from different companies, were very much aligned in their remarks. They both stated plainly and clearly that they wanted the salespeople they worked with to help them tackle the big issues and challenges. What was most interesting was that both started by talking about catastrophic failure.

The first executive said, "At some point, you will have a catastrophic failure. It's not a matter of if, it's a matter of when. We want to talk about what we need to do when you, our partner, have an issue that harms our business. We want to know what you are going to need us to do when that happens." This type of catastrophic failure is something that every company fears, especially when their clients may not be able to operate for some time when it occurs. This is exactly the thing that salespeople are afraid to address, as talking about a failure means that there are risks in working with them and their company.

I am using this example to make a point about what gives one an executive presence and what subtracts from that outcome. The willingness to talk about the systemic problems and challenges in producing results together is what makes you a strategic partner, a trusted adviser, and someone with an executive presence. Avoiding those conversations and pretending that systemic problems and challenges don't exist is what causes your dream client to look elsewhere for good counsel.

As you already know from earlier chapters, these unaddressed systemic problems and challenges are what cause companies to change partners. Your dream client is likely already working with someone who doesn't want to address the problems or challenges that prevent them from getting the results they need. Maybe they lack the resourcefulness to come up with new ideas, or maybe they are avoiding issues they believe would lose them support, having been around long enough to be an actor in their client's internal politics.

When I first started selling staffing, almost every one of my competitors would tell their clients that they would never have no-shows. In other words, they would never face a situation where an assigned employee would show up for work one day and then disappear the next (or in some cases, never show up at all). These were low-wage employees, and the companies they were assigned to made no real commitment to them. The contract was out of balance; you work for me as long as I need you, and when I don't need you, I let you go.

In contrast, rather than telling clients that they would never have no-shows, I insisted they would. I explained to them that their low pay rate and low commitment all but guaranteed they would be missing people, and that we would have to work very hard to keep their positions filled, even sending people in on days they didn't want to have to train people. I told the truth, and I spoke as someone with experience, authority, and a good bit of resourcefulness. The result of this interaction was that I was awarded the business, and I attribute that to my willingness to tell the truth, even when the client wasn't thrilled to hear it.

BE A PEER, NOT AN ORDER-TAKER

Let's be clear: You are your dream client's peer. Having informed opinions and a point of view, having information that the client doesn't have, being comfortable with conflict, and dealing with real challenges and problems all help to make you a peer, while massively differentiating you from your competitors—including their current partner.

The opposite of a peer is the order-taker. The order-taker cares deeply about being liked. They are concerned about not doing or saying anything that may prevent their prospective clients from giving them an order. If they had a point of view about the client's business that was in conflict with the client's existing beliefs, they would never speak it out loud for fear of damaging the relationship. The order-taker also knows little besides their products and services, their features and benefits, and how to take an order. They would never so much as hint at an issue, like a buyer making a bad decision or underinvesting in the results they need. The order-taker avoids conflict at all costs, and this conflict aversion eliminates the possibility of being a peer, being consultative, or being a trusted adviser.

Stated more simply, you can't be a subservient, conflict-averse knownothing.

DO THIS NOW

1. What is your informed opinion and your point of view about what your dream clients should be doing now to produce better results?

2. What do you know so well that your client can completely depend on you to keep them educated, and what do you need to share with them now?

To download the worksheet that accompanies this chapter, go to www.eattheirlunch.training.

Chapter 12

HOW TO BUILD A WALL OF FIRE AROUND YOUR CLIENTS

WINNING NEW CLIENTS ISN'T ENOUGH. YOU ALSO HAVE TO RE-
tain them, and you have to help them grow so you can grow with them.
Focusing on their continued growth is the only way to avoid slipping into
the complacency that opens you up to the risk of being competitively displaced.

It's important to remember that while you are pursuing your dream
clients and working to take them away from your competitors, your competitors are not sitting idle. Your competitors are right now doing the same
thing and pursuing your clients. One of the factors that prevents your
growth is churn, where you lose clients faster than you gain them. While
you are executing the plays in this competitive displacement playbook, you
have to protect your existing clients. There is one major retention strategy
that causes salespeople to produce results that are something less than
they are capable of.

OUTCOMES, TRANSACTIONS, AND MOTHER HENS

A mother hen sits on her eggs until they hatch. She keeps them warm, and
she protects them from threats. She's good at keeping her eggs warm, but

being a mother hen, she's not so great at protecting them from external threats and predators. Being a "mother hen" in sales means sitting on your own accounts and trying to protect them from harm instead of prospecting and creating new opportunities, and doing the real work that retains clients. Where salespeople go wrong is believing that because they sold the client a set of outcomes, they own the transactions that produce the outcomes. What does that mean? Consider the following situations:

- If there is a problem with an order, the salesperson is Johnny-on-the-spot or Jenny-on-the-spot. They track down the missing order, follow up with the shipping company, call their customer service team, and move heaven and earth to find that order.
- When an invoice is incorrect, the salesperson gets a copy from the client and one from their billing department and sits down at their computer to create an invoice template in a spreadsheet and correct it themselves. All this despite the fact that the salesperson is no designer, struggles with Excel, and has a tough time figuring out the invoice themselves.
- When the client needs reports, they reach out to the salesperson to make a request. The salesperson, feeling the need to prove their heroism in serving the client, generates the reports the client needs to make sure that everything is just so. To be on the safe side, they also build a slide deck of charts so that the client will be doubly impressed.

These are all transactions. They are things that need to be done to serve the client. But they are not the outcome that the salesperson sold the client. The outcome they sold was a better future state, one where the client generated higher revenue, higher profit, lower costs, increased market share, exploited a new and untapped market, resolved a throughput issue that had gone unaddressed for five years, or massively transformed some part of their operation.

The problems that come along with the day-to-day service of the account do not belong to you, the salesperson. They belong to your team. Your job in sales can be boiled down to two things: opportunity creation and opportunity capture. You need to ensure that your client obtains the outcomes you sell, and you are responsible for that because that is what you sold. Without ensuring that you deliver the results you sold, you decrease the chances of creating and winning the next opportunity with that client. How could it be otherwise? You told them they'd receive a specific outcome and that didn't happen. Why would next time be different?

When the client calls and asks for help with an order, your role is to listen to the client, assess the problem, and then tell them that you are going to give the information to someone on your operation team who will call them to ensure that they have all the details. You also tell the client that your team is outstanding, they will resolve the problem, and they will keep you both informed of their progress. Then you promise to call them back by the end of the day to make sure your team resolved the problem to their satisfaction. After you have done this, which should cost you all of ten minutes, you go back to doing work that creates greater outcomes, trusting your team to take care of the transactions.

But the problem with owning the transactions in the bullet points above is more important than those examples make it out to be. By believing these transactions will protect your client from a competitive displacement, you are failing to do the real work necessary to build a wall of fire around your client.

HOW TO RETAIN YOUR DREAM CLIENT

If solving the day-to-day challenges your client faces isn't enough to retain them, what is? What is necessary to prevent being displaced?

New Value

From quarter to quarter and year to year, you have to create new value proactively. Creating new value requires that you look at your client's business as a strategic partner, develop a roadmap for better future results, and continually make a case for future change.

Earlier in this book we looked at some of the reasons your competitor may have put themselves in a place where a competitive displacement was possible—or even certain. Things like complacency, apathy, unaddressed systemic challenges, or service issues all open your client up to being stolen out from underneath you. The very best and surest way to protect against any of these things is the continual creation of new value.

What got you here, in this case, will get you there. When you won your dream client, you showed up with a compelling reason for your client to change. You built consensus around that change. You worked to help the client move forward, and you helped them produce the better results they needed. All of these actions that allowed you to win the client's business make up the exact and exacting recipe for retention.

Instead of busying yourself with transactions, chasing down orders, typing invoices, and generating reports (or picking up their dry cleaning, walking their dogs, or picking up milk and bread from the corner store), you focus on creating new value. You work on building the next opportunity, the next initiative that will drive even better results. If you are going to spend time with your existing client, then you have to create value for them during that time. One of the best ways for you to think about this work is the idea of a roadmap. Where are you taking your dream client over the next thirty-six months? Let's say they start buying from you in the first quarter of a year. You spend a quarter getting them up and running, and a quarter fine-tuning whatever it is you do to make it hum. What comes after that? Once they are up and running and generating new outcomes, what do they need to do next to perform even better? Maybe that second initiative takes six months to implement fully. What comes after that?

If you were to sit down with a pen and a piece of paper right now, drawing twelve quarters across the top of the page, what would you list under those quarters as initiatives that would cause your client to change and create greater value and even more exceptional outcomes for them? If you can draw that on a piece of paper, you have a roadmap. In thirty-six months, there will be new challenges and events that compel change. As long as you stay vigilant and continue to survey the landscape, remain close to the stakeholders to understand the changes they need to make, and work to create new opportunities, you can block competitive threats.

The primary key to retention is to go from quarter to quarter and year to year always pushing to create new value. If there is a compelling reason to change, you will initiate that change, and by doing so prevent your dream client from having to entertain your competitor's big idea, the one that would give rise to your displacement. One of the primary attributes of sales organizations and salespeople who create greater value is this future orientation. Instead of passively reacting to a client's request for change, you proactively make a case for change. Compelling change is the difference between Level 3 and Level 4 when it comes to value creation. The way you slip from Level 4 to Level 3 is by growing complacent and waiting passively for your client to say "Jump!" You need to be already jumping, presenting the case for change, always moving things forward.

If you want to be your dream client's strategic partner, then you must act like you are a member of their leadership team. You have to bring them the new ideas, the changes they need to make, the "what comes next."

Accountability for Results

Protecting your clients from competitive threats starts with owning the outcomes you sell. You must be accountable for producing the results you promise, making adjustments, resolving issues, and ensuring execution. Greater ownership creates greater loyalty. If your dream client can count on you to deliver some outcome, they can direct their attention to other things, knowing you will take care of what is yours.

There are two mistakes we must look at when it comes to retaining your dream clients and protecting them from external threats. The first is not being accountable for the results you sell and failing your dream clients. The second is not taking credit for the results you produce.

The fastest way to create a gap in performance so big that your competitor can walk right through it and steal your dream client away is to avoid being accountable for the results you produce. The failure to execute puts your dream client in the position of having to look elsewhere to find the partner they need. You may have the business acumen and situational knowledge. You may have the very best of ideas. You may be able to build consensus around an idea, charming even the most obstinate of all opponents, getting everyone to "yes" at the same time and winning a deal. But all of this is for naught if you can't execute what you sell. When your client can't run their business because what you are doing is preventing them from doing it, they're forced to do what is necessary to produce the results they promise their clients and customers. If your lack of execution costs them time and money, they have to be responsible to their company and their team and remedy your failing.

Your relationship cannot cause your client to lose theirs. They can't destroy their relationships with the people on their teams by protecting your lack of execution. Nor can they lose clients and customers because of your failings. But I want to be clear here that we are talking about the failure to execute, not the challenges that come with execution. You will have difficulties performing for your client, just as they have problems and challenges serving their clients. The challenges, however, cannot be allowed to go on forever. They have to be addressed and dispatched.

The tenth commitment in *The Lost Art of Closing* is the commitment to execute. Most people believe the commitment to buy is the final decision the buyer needs to make, but it isn't. They have to commit to executing. That chapter of the book covers two ideas, the first of which is that you will have to work inside your organization to make the necessary changes to execute for your client when you struggle to produce results. That internal sale to your team and management can be difficult, but it is crucial. Equally important is the client's commitment to execute on their side. Some of the challenges in execution occur when your client doesn't pick up their end of the stick, meaning you are doing what is necessary while they refuse to change what they need to change on their side, even though they agreed to do so. You have to intervene and help them make those changes, lest you open yourself up to a displacement—even if it is your client's lack of execution that is the cause.

Which brings us to another threat to retention, and that is not taking credit for the results you are producing. There are absolute laws of working with clients that go like this:

- The client will remember and recall every problem, challenge, or issue they've had to endure over the course of your relationship with 10× greater clarity than they will every time you've resolved a problem, challenge, or issue for them.
- The client will not know how well you are doing executing and generating the results you promised.

In school, a 97 percent grade is an A. In some schools it might even be an A+. Your client, however, is likely to focus on just the 3 percent where you aren't performing—unless you point them to everything you've done to get to 97 percent. Which is why it is important that you keep your own score and grade yourself, sharing your internal score with your client. You must provide proof that you are executing, so when someone asks your contacts how you are doing, they can defend you and your results.

Start by taking credit for how well you are executing. Then recount the problems and challenges you've had, acknowledging any failures and sharing how you've rectified them. If there are still gaps, make sure your client knows you are aware of them, what you are doing about them, and when you expect to resolve them completely. If the problems require your client to change something they're doing, a meeting to review your scores is a good time to have that conversation.

If no one knows what you are doing, you are not doing anything. This is as true of your challenges as it is of your successes. Keep your own score and eliminate the need for your client to do so.

Developing and Protecting Relationships

The fewer people who know, like, trust, and find value in you and your team, the higher the risk of your being competitively displaced. When events occur, like a larger company buying your client's company or your key stakeholder leaving, you need relationships with people who will defend you and fight to keep you. This requires that you develop relationships horizontally and vertically throughout the organization.

If you have been playing the great game of sales for any amount of time, you have had the unfortunate experience of having a contact who gave you her full support, protecting you from any threats and ensuring that you retained her company's business, leave and be replaced with a change agent. Your contact's replacement, needing an early win and a chance to establish themselves as a change agent, surveys the landscape to discover a supplier (you are not a strategic partner as far as they are concerned) who has a number of current challenges delivering a result they need. Without understanding that the problems are systemic and might be the result of the company's unwillingness to change, even though you have recommended that change no less than ten times, the new contact decides to remove the supplier and replace them with a company they used in their last role.

In many cases, a new leader finds that removing a supplier is easier than removing a person who works for the company. The supplier may or may not have deep relationships, but even if they do, it's just a supplier. Suppliers are easy to come by, and swapping one for another isn't the end of the world. Not knowing the political landscape, this is more attractive than letting go of an employee who has deep relationships with the rest of their team. That decision comes with more risk because the new leader doesn't know who will see that decision as being harmful.

This is why it is dangerous to rely on a single sponsor who is willing to support you when a potentially adverse event occurs. Events will occur over the lifetime of serving a client. Your sponsor will leave to take another job or retire. Your client's company will be purchased by another company that already has a contract with a company they consider to be their strategic partner. There will be some initiative to review all contracts, putting them all out to bid, just to keep everyone honest. Or some competitive salesperson will find their way into the building through some little crack you've left open and provide their contact with a proposal with a price tag that is 33 percent less than your pricing. (I faced this when one of my company's competitors sent their pricing proposal to everyone in the leadership team of my client's company as a way to put us on our back foot. We had the relationships to survive. Barely.)

So when something happens, you want more than one person within your dream client's company who will go to the mat to defend you. You want as many people as possible with influence fighting to keep you because you are an essential and integral part of what they are doing and losing you would be too heavy a price to pay. The more people who believe that you are a strategic partner (Level 4), the more who will be willing to defend you. Equally, the more people with influence who think you create a low level of value, say, the commodity level of value that is Level 1, the less likely it is that they will defend you, and the less ammunition they will have to do so. This is true even when the end users appreciate your Level 1 value.

You might be tempted to think that the stakeholders whose support you need must be at the top of the organizational chart. It is not always true. Much of the time, the people who execute and rely on you and your solutions have very low formal authority and exceptionally high influence. They can make it very difficult to remove you by explaining why you are essential, leaning on their subject matter expertise to defend you and your solution.

Developing relationships that will withstand any threat of competitive displacement isn't easy. All relationships come with a price. That price is time and energy. Paying that price means having a presence and being engaged. It requires intimacy. You have to know the people you work with, who they are, what they want, why they want it, what they prefer, and what they don't want. Intimacy means: you know me, you understand me, you get me. If you don't know me, understand me, and get me, then I am going to be open to relationships with other people who do. If you don't care enough to develop a relationship with me, then I'll look to someone else who does. If you do know me, understand me, and get me, that intimacy will cause me to defend you from all comers, because change comes with too high a risk when it comes to my getting what I want, how I want it.

Relationships are necessary to retain your clients and protect yourself from a competitive displacement. Let's look at the practical "how to" part of this approach.

Establishing a Cadence

You can protect your clients from risk by developing a cadence to your relationship. One of the best ways to do so is with quarterly business reviews, but it is also important to establish the beats between those major meetings. Let's look at what you can and should do to make sure you build a wall of fire around your clients.

Let's start here with big periodic meetings, like quarterly business reviews with your clients. A QBR is a big meeting with the contacts and leadership team of your client companies where you get a chance to report your score, discuss issues and their resolutions, and discuss future changes. It allows you to deepen relationships, share your score, and create new value. Because the agenda is valuable for your client's executive leadership team and the stakeholders you work with day-to-day, you have the opportunity to get many of your contacts in the same room. Your client's leadership team may have no idea what you are doing, what kind of challenges you're having, what kind of changes you have made over the prior quarter, how well you are doing, or what you are recommending that you do together next. If you don't share these things with them, they may perceive you as doing nothing. If you don't share your new ideas and insights, you open up the possibility of a competitor sharing their bias and point of view, one that may capture mindshare. Moreover, if you aren't listening to your client's leadership team, you won't know what they consider to be their highest priorities, nor will you know what you should be changing on your side to help them.

These meetings are major beats. There need to be minor beats between these beats to develop and deepen the relationships. Those minor beats might be weekly coordinating meetings or calls with the people on your team, followed by monthly review calls with you to ensure that you are producing the outcomes you sold and promised (with a stern reminder here that you don't own the transactions).

Other minor beats might be meetings with your client's management team to share ideas about what comes next in an environment where it is safe to explore and where doing so won't rile up the rest of the stakeholders. When you are proposing new value, you are proposing change. That means you'll need to repeat the consensus-building work you did to win the client in the first place, and that may require that you seed the idea carefully, getting all the friendlies onboard first.

Everything in this chapter is what you need to do to build an impenetrable wall of fire around your dream clients, resting assured that they are safe from competitive displacements while you do the work of displacing your competitors.

DO THIS NOW

1. What new value do you need to create for your existing clients to protect them from competitive threats?

2. Create a scorecard to share with your clients to remind them of the value you create for them—and how well you are solving their problems and challenges.

   To download the worksheet that accompanies this chapter, go to www.eattheirlunch.training.

Conclusion

PARTING THOUGHTS

IN A WORLD THAT IS INCREASINGLY CONCERNED WITH TRANS-
actions instead of relationships, the competitive advantage will go to those
who invest in human relations, deep connections, and the serving of other
human beings.

Right now, the great push in sales is to automate everything, especially prospecting. Because the B2C world is now thriving on selling in a
way where the customer can just click to buy what they may want or need
without human interaction, many sales leaders and their executive leadership teams in the B2B world would like to reduce the cost of acquiring
clients by following this same model. Although these sales leaders and
executives are increasingly concerned about being perceived as commodities, they make a decision to do something that increases the perception of
commoditization, that demonstrates a lack of differentiation, and that creates little to no value for the prospective clients. This makes these leaders
no different from the purchasing agent who doesn't recognize the difference between price and cost. By attempting to lower the price of acquiring
a new client, they increase the cost by behaving as if this outcome is a
transaction—when it is anything but a transaction to the dream client
who is being asked to fire their current supplier. You are always better off

paying in full for what you want than looking for a deal and underinvesting in your desired result. If you would accuse your clients of stepping over dollars to pick up dimes, don't be guilty of doing the same.

Eat Their Lunch, another book with a provocative title, is my third attempt at pushing back against the prevailing winds. As quixotic as this effort might seem, those of us who still believe in human relationships and thrive on the opportunity to help others create change and produce better results will be on the winning side of this argument in the long run. When what a person or organization buys requires a significant investment of time, energy, and resources—especially when it is central to producing some strategic result—human relationships will always be crucial. As the business world gets pulled in two directions, super transactional and super relational, you will find real value and differentiation by moving toward super relational and away from transacting.

Because of the technical nature of a lot of what we sell, there are more engineers today filling the role of salesperson and subject matter expert (or SME). In the future, we are likely to see this trend matched with salespeople—and leaders—with liberal arts, master of fine arts, and humanities degrees, something that seems to be missing in much of Silicon Valley. The more things are made by machine, sold by computer, and communicated through chat bots, the more valuable a relationship with a person who cares will become.

The ideas that I've shared in this book, starting with the need to help your prospective clients change and produce better results, form an imperative that comes from caring. It comes from having insight and putting it to work on behalf of your clients. If you want purpose and meaning in your work, this is where you'll find it. If you want to find the inspiration that propels you out of bed in the morning, being of service, making a contribution, and making a difference for other people is as worthy a charge as any.

The middle section of the book, which helps you understand your clients and prospective clients by viewing them through some new, sharper lenses, deepens your understanding of the people you are working to help. It provides a more holistic view of what is necessary to move them to a better future state.

The final third of the book is dedicated to the idea that you need to improve who you are to improve what you do, and it aligns with the idea that relationships matter, despite the many forces that are pushing to automate and commoditize everything in sight. Right now there is no greater imperative than your own personal and professional growth. That is the core message of all my books. Your dream client is deciding whom to trust, whom to buy from, and whom to add to their team. When we lose deals, we want to blame our pricing, our competitor, or the client. But no matter how you try to absolve yourself of responsibility for the loss, if the wins are yours, so are the losses.

If you've read this far, I know something about you. You are the kind of person who cares about their personal and professional development. You want to arm yourself with the mind-set, skill sets, and tool kits to create a competitive advantage and do your best work. Competitive displacements are not easy to pull off, but because you have read this book and are putting it to work, you will succeed where others fail, and you will acquire new clients that are presently being served (albeit not as well as they should be) by your competitors.

You are prepared to create a higher level of value for the person sitting across the table from you. You are the one who is super relational in a world where people are treated like a transaction. You're also the one who decides that the people you serve can be complicated, messy, difficult to serve, hard to understand, and still worth the investment of your time and energy.

You also decide to create value for that individual by giving them your presence. By listening to them. By trying to understand how to help them and all the people on their team, even though you know it won't be easy.

By working with them, even though it won't be as fast as you wish it were, and even in a world where some relationships are measured in clicks and likes and emojis, you are the person who shows up. You are the person who has a physical presence and looks their prospective clients in the eyes, even though there are now media available that would save you the time and trouble.

The opportunity to do your best work, the work that gives your life purpose and meaning, won't be found in clicks or likes or retweets or what you share on social media sites. The work you do that will make a difference will be the work you do with other people to help them with their challenges. If this strikes you as something outside of commercial enterprise, and if you believe that this has no application to the business you're in, let me help you reframe your thoughts about what we do.

Much of our lives is spent at work. If you've read this far, I'm guessing most of your life is spent with your clients and prospective clients. The decision as to whether or not to give your whole self to that endeavor, to infuse your interactions with sincere caring and the goal of making a difference for another human being, is wholly within your power. The decision to treat someone like something more than a transaction, like a human being that you care for, is a decision you make each time you sit down across from your prospective client or clients. I don't pretend that there aren't days when it is easier to go through the motions. I know that when you have bills to pay, kids to take care of, a household to run, demanding clients, and the coming end of quarter when you are behind your quota, it can be difficult to give your whole self over to your work. I know it is hard; I've felt it myself. But the decision to push back against that feeling, to give another human being and their challenges your full focus, is the differentiator worth acknowledging.

In a business where creating a preference to work with you is probably the single most significant determining factor of your success, it's the human things that will make a difference and tilt that scale in favor of you over any and all others who do less. Doing less than this, transacting, is the fastest path to being disintermediated. It's also the quickest path to finding your work to be meaningless and to have no value. Transacting is how we lose our sense of connection, our sense of community, our sense of duty and obligation to one another.

This book is a field manual. It's designed to help you displace your competitor by creating greater value for your prospective and dream clients than anyone else. I hope that I can implore you to do this work in the spirit with which I wrote this book. Every Sunday, I end my weekly newsletter with the words "Do good work." These words speak to the quality of the work we do, but also our intentions.

Do good work and email me your success stories at anthony@iannarino.com.

ACKNOWLEDGMENTS

The release date for this book is almost exactly two years from the release date of my first book, *The Only Sales Guide You'll Ever Need*, with *The Lost Art of Closing* being released ten months later. That makes writing a gratitude section both incredibly easy and incredibly difficult at the same time. Easy because the cast of characters hasn't changed much. Difficult because none of this work would exist without their continued support.

Cher, for your patience. Aidan, for your confidence. Mia, for your sense of justice. Ava, for your raw determination. Mom, for your unwavering values and support. Dad, for your belief. Thada, for your ability to develop relationships. Tara, for being able to connect with people faster than anyone. Jason, for helping people laugh at themselves in difficult times, me especially. Mike, for being my partner in high crimes and misdemeanors.

My family at Solutions Staffing and Iannarino Fullen Group, especially Peg Mativi and Geoff Fullen.

Adrian Zackheim, Will Weisser, Kaushik Viswanath, Alyssa Adler, and Katherine Valentino at Portfolio Penguin Random House, for your belief in my work and your help with both of my books. My friends at 800CEOREAD.

ACKNOWLEDGMENTS

Very special thanks to the Titans, Jeb Blount, Mark Hunter, and Mike Weinberg.

Seth Godin for his example, his inspiration, and his wisdom.

Beth Mastre, Heather May, Francesco Lazzerro, Damian Wohrer, Dave Gardner, Amber Hersch, Bob Cabarcas, Zach Hoover, Gwen Cecil, Amy Tobin, Justin Levrier, Taylor Bennett, Hunter Myers.

Nathan Speiser, Patrick Gallagher, Jim Bostick, David Lawrence, Steve Malvesta, Jeff Smith, Brittany Francis, Carsten Michaelis, Ivan Tachiev, John Pecaric, Jim Marks, Al Dupont, Steve Finzer, Tim Methenitis, Dan Perrone, Stacey Clevenger, Steve Byrne, Terri Kachinsky, Sarah Kilburg, Steve Sassman, David Neenan, Rick Marcet, Sean Diamond, Christina Ritchie, Bryan Thomas, Brian Yarmowich, Bill Proctor, Ricky Arriola, Jason Schlenker, Dan Arriola, Christina Canizares, John Watkins, Jay Herther, John LaBrosse, Cosmo Mazza, Jim Hartigan, Sue Downer, Mark Gibson, Mike Sheridan, Price Burlington, Fred Page, Alan Martin, Rich Nigro, Stacey Curry, Brandon Humphrey, Andy Schuster, Amir Nizam, Riad Nizam, Jamil Nizam, Jodie Boeldt, Leigha Schatzman, Isabela Bray, Judy Toland, Molly Hallahan, Cliff Albert, Greg Jones, and Kyle Rowe.

Carrie Martinez, Lahat Tzvi, Miles Austin, John Spence, Mike Kunkle, Leann Hoagland Smith, Matt Heinz, Lori Richardson, Tibor Shanto, Alen Mayer, Bob Terson, Karin Bellantoni, Kelley Robertson, Todd Schnick, Alice R. Heiman, Gary Hart, Nancy Nardin, Andy Paul, Steven Rosen, Elinor Stutz, Richard Ruff and Janet Spirer, Dianna Gearin, Deb Calvert, Jack Malcolm, Jeff Beals, Jim Keenan, Babbette Ten Haken, Dan Waldschmidt, Tim Ohai, Kelly Riggs, Dorian Lynn Hidy, Doyle Slayton, Lee Bartlett, Kelly McCormick, Dave Brock, Gerhard Gschwandtner, Bob Burg, Douglas Burdette, Michael Flynn, Donald Kelly, Phil Gerbyshak, Dave Savage, Anthony Conklin, James Carbary, Will Barron, and Paul Watts.

INDEX

Page numbers of illustrations appear in italics.

INDEX

Also by Anthony Iannarino

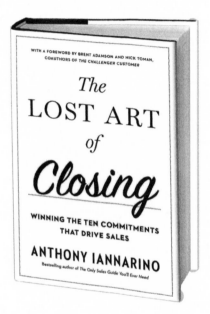

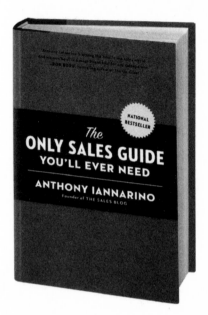

TheSalesBlog.com

PORTFOLIO
PENGUIN